A Year of
Gratitude

Publications International, Ltd.

Let's get social!

 @Publications_International

 @PublicationsInternational

www.pilbooks.com

Table of Contents

Introduction

When we open our hearts to God, we see the ways his many blessings flow through us and imbue our lives with love and guidance. Sometimes, however, his grace is difficult to find. In times of doubt and anger, God seems distant from us. We become easily overwhelmed by our obligations, focusing on pain and hardship. Take comfort in your faith and remember that God will never abandon you. Find his loving presence all around you, in the ground beneath your feet, the warming sun on your face, and the gentle music of his songbirds.

A Year of Gratitude is a daily guide to help refocus your faith as you express your feelings of thanks and appreciation toward God. Throughout this book, you'll find verses, reflections, and prayers for every day of the calendar year. Recognize that God is guiding you on your journey, and open your eyes to all that he has to offer. Be thankful for his many blessings and welcome each and every day with gratitude.

January

This is the day which the Lord hath made; we will rejoice and be glad in it.

—Psalm 118:24

Wake up in the morning and be grateful for the new day ahead. Every 24 hours is an opportunity to live life more fully, and love more deeply. Look at each moment and see the gift it brings. Cherish the present as it unfolds. Then, when you go to sleep at night, be thankful for the experiences God gave you. This is a life well-lived.

A new heart also will I give you, and a new spirit will I put within you: and I will take away the stony heart out of your flesh, and I will give you an heart of flesh.

—Ezekiel 36:26

Lord, sometimes I get frustrated, especially when I have to face something new. Thank you for giving me an open heart. Help me accept change and rejoice in new experiences and new people. Help me to be grateful for new opportunities and always see the good things even when I am afraid to try something new.

My God shall supply all your need according to his riches in glory by Christ Jesus.

—Philippians 4:19

Lord, I open my eyes and all I see are the amazing blessings that surround me. In this moment, I want for nothing, and I live with the knowledge that I can always turn to you for help, and cast my cares upon you, when my clarity and my vision cloud with worry. Thank you, Lord, for reminding me that the joyful blessings of this moment are all because of your love for me.

Behold, God is my salvation; I will trust, and not be afraid: for the Lord Jehovah is my strength and my song; he also is become my salvation.

—Isaiah 12:2

Sometimes I try to do too much "building" and "guarding" by my own efforts, Father. Thank you for this reminder that everything I do to further my own cause and ensure my own safety isn't going to be effective apart from an abiding trust in you. Help me remember, too, that you aren't just an element of my life, like some add-on magic charm to hedge all my bets. Forgive me for the times I've treated you like that! You're no optional feature. You are my provision and my protection—you are my very life. Thank you for the peace of mind that always comes when I stop trying to do it myself and tap into your unending supply of strength.

Cause me to hear thy lovingkindness in the morning; for in thee do I trust: cause me to know the way wherein I should walk; for I lift up my soul unto thee.

—Psalm 143:8

Lord, how blessed we are to be able to see you all around us and to sense your presence within us. Even though we can't see you in the same way we might see a friend or a neighbor, we see you in your Word and in all that is good and true in the world around us. Thank you, Lord, for making yourself so available to us.

> Great peace
> have they which
> love thy law: and
> nothing shall
> offend them.
>
> —Psalm 119:165

Dear God,

Your peace is like the sweet calm air after a storm, like a warm blanket on a cold winter day, like a happy smile of someone I love on a day when nothing has gone right. Your peace brings me the comfort and the strength I need to get through the hardest of times and the thickest of situations. I am so grateful, God, for the kind of peace your presence offers me, a peace so deep and abiding I know that no matter what is happening, that peace is there for me to tap into. Like an overflowing well at the center of my being, your presence is the water that quenches my thirst and gives me renewed vigor and life. Thank you, God, for your everlasting peace. Amen.

For he saith to the snow, Be thou on the earth; likewise to the small rain, and to the great rain of his strength.

—Job 37:6

Sometimes it is difficult to appreciate snowy weather, but I thank God for the gift of snow days. How wonderful it is for everyone to be home, safe and warm. On snow days, life returns to a simpler pace and the demands of schedules and responsibilities fall away. Thank you, Lord, for the beauty of the snow and the time it gives us to relax and share quiet times with our loved ones.

Thou art more glorious and excellent than the mountains of prey.

—Psalm 76:4

Almighty God, do we tell you often enough how awesome you are? We stand before you in complete awe of your creation, your sovereignty, and your power. Let us never minimize the ability you have to change our reality in an instant, even when it involves moving mountains or calming storms. You, O God, are the one and only God, and we give you glory at all times. Thank you for your strengthening presence in our lives.

I will instruct thee and teach thee in the way which thou shalt go: I will guide thee with mine eye.

—Psalm 32:8

Enid's faith helps her as she pursues the dream of opening a bookstore. "I've wanted to run a bookshop since I was little," she says. "I used to go to the independent bookstore in my hometown; it was an important place in my childhood. Now I'm opening my own shop, in the town where I went to college." Is she scared? "Sometimes," she says. "But I feel like God is guiding me in my decisions. That gives me courage."

Dear Lord, thank you for guiding me as I dream of great things.

For the Lord giveth wisdom: out of his mouth cometh knowledge and understanding.

—Proverbs 2:6

Lord, your Word is so alive—so vibrant—that it almost seems illuminated when I am reading it. When I am troubled, opening the Bible is like turning on a comforting light in a dark, gloomy room. Thank you, Lord, for loving us so much that you gave us your wisdom to illuminate our lives.

Let your light so shine before men, that they may see your good works, and glorify your Father which is in heaven.

—Matthew 5:16

God, thank you for giving me this light of mine to shine. I promise never to conceal the brilliance you've bestowed upon me. May I forever reflect the glow of your loving presence. Amen.

> The fear of man bringeth a snare: but whoso putteth his trust in the Lord shall be safe.
>
> —Proverbs 29:25

Dear Lord,

Thank you for the courage you've given me to pursue my dreams. So many of my friends have settled for lives filled with regrets and unfulfilled dreams, and I've been so blessed by you with the inner fire and drive to take my divinely-given talents and do something with them. No matter how hard I worked, I knew that I could not achieve such goals without you and I've always strived to keep your presence close at hand in all my decisions and choices. Thank you, Lord, for helping me find that extra strength within to face my fears, my doubts, and my insecurities and go for a life well-lived. Amen.

The Lord is my strength and my shield; my heart trusted in him, and I am helped: therefore my heart greatly rejoiceth; and with my song will I praise him.

—Psalm 28:7

Father, when I don't have another ounce of strength to give, you give me gallons of love to fuel my spirit. When I think I can't continue, you push me further and steady my steps. Thank you, God.

And it came to pass, that, while they communed together and reasoned, Jesus himself drew near, and went with them.

—Luke 24:15

Father God,

You send us companions on our journey to you—we walk this path with all those who seek you. Like Cleopas and his companion on the road to Emmaus, we talk together, share our stories, and try to discern the presence of Jesus in our lives. Thank you for those you send to be spiritual support!

Lord, you've given me a great team of helpers,

And I'm exceedingly thankful.

Where would I be without them?

They seem to know my needs before I do,

And they jump to meet them.

I know you've given them those gifts of caring,

Of encouragement, of hospitality and healing,

But they're using those gifts as you intended,

To show your love to others—I mean me.

I am thankful to you and to them.

There's not much I can do to pay them back, Lord.

They'd probably refuse a reward anyway.

So I ask you to shower them with blessings,

Just as they have brought blessing to me.

Give them joy and peace in rich supply,

And let your love continue to flow

To them, within them, and through them.

Amen.

And blessed is she that believed: for there shall be a performance of those things which were told her from the Lord.

—Luke 1:45

Our relationships strengthen us. This came home to me the other day, when an exchange with a coworker left me feeling irresolute and unsettled. During my commute home, my stomach was in knots: I went over and over the disagreement in my head. It was hard to sort out whether I'd handled things with grace. When I got home, I found that my husband had started dinner; the warm atmosphere of love and regard unclenched my heart, and I was able to talk frankly about the day. My husband's nonjudgmental but clear-sighted perspective helped me sort how to remedy the situation; after we talked, we took a moment to pray together. God, thank you for reminding us of the importance of believing: in you, and in one another.

Be kindly affectioned one to another with brotherly love; in honour preferring one another.

—Romans 12:10

Heavenly Father, we are thankful for family. Please bring our family together in happiness. Help us see everything as your children do: with wonder and awe. Glorious are your creations! Thank you for creating us. We love our family. We love you. Amen.

> O give thanks unto the Lord; for he is good; for his mercy endureth for ever.
>
> —1 Chronicles 16:34

God of all comfort, have mercy on me. I got angry today at my husband and accused him of not helping me enough. I scolded my child for talking too much. I shouted at the dog for barking too loud. And I almost hung up on my neighbor for taking up too much of my time with her plumbing problems. I need your comforting strength, dear God, wrapped around me like a soothing blanket, so that I can ask my family for forgiveness. Bless me with more patience, too, so that we don't have to go through all this again tomorrow. Thank you, God.

When pride cometh, then cometh shame: but with the lowly is wisdom.

—Proverbs 11:2

Here we are again, Lord. Another time when I feel like I've made a complete mess of this life you've given me. I place myself in your hands. If you need to totally reshape me to turn me into someone more useful, so be it! Thank you for not abandoning me, your humble creation. Make me over in your design.

Whither shall I go from thy spirit? or whither shall I flee from thy presence?

—Psalm 139:7

Lord, you know me. Sometimes, that thought is intimidating. I don't want you to see all my flaws and foibles! I become discouraged by the thought of how petty I must seem to you, how earthly my concerns. I think that if you truly know me, you'll think me unworthy of your love.

But I know you do love me! You alone can both fully know me and fully love me. I thank you for that incredible gift.

When ye pray, say, Our Father which art in heaven, Hallowed be thy name. Thy kingdom come. Thy will be done, as in heaven, so in earth. Give us day by day our daily bread. And forgive us our sins; for we also forgive every one that is indebted to us. And lead us not into temptation; but deliver us from evil.

—Luke 11:2-4

Lord, thank you for the gift of prayer. What an amazing gift it is to be able to speak to you any time I need to. May I remember to not only seek you in times of need, but to thank you for all the blessings in my life. May my time in prayer bring me closer to you and help me be grateful for all the wonderful things in my life.

All the while my breath is in me, and the spirit of God is in my nostrils; My lips shall not speak wickedness, nor my tongue utter deceit.

—Job 27:3-4

Lord, with each breath I take I am aware that it is you who breathed life into me. My next breath is as dependent on you as my last breath was. And I can confidently rest in the knowledge that it will be you and you alone who will determine when the last breath leaves my body and I go to be with you. Today, Lord, I thank you for the gift of life and for each breath I take.

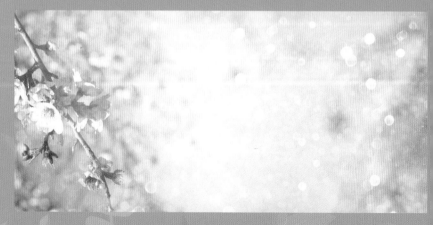

Take therefore no thought for the morrow: for the morrow shall take thought for the things of itself. Sufficient unto the day is the evil thereof.

—Matthew 6:34

Lord, even though I know worry is a useless waste of time and energy, it snares me again and again. Thank you for helping me notice early on that I'm about to wallow in worry once more. As I give this situation to you, Lord, I release my need to worry about it as well. Instead, I look for the blessings in the midst of all that's going on and thank you wholeheartedly for them. I willingly trade my worry for your peace.

Let us therefore come boldly unto the throne of grace, that we may obtain mercy, and find grace to help in time of need.

—Hebrews 4:16

Lord, once again I am aware that you, by your grace, gave me the strength to work through a situation that I was woefully unprepared to face. I accept that when we are completely out of ideas, drained of all energy, and so sick at heart we can barely breathe, your grace and strength lift us up and carry us forward. Thank you, Lord.

And his fame went throughout all Syria: and they brought unto him all sick people that were taken with divers diseases and torments, and those which were possessed with devils, and those which were lunatick, and those that had the palsy; and he healed them.

—Matthew 4:24

We don't really know why we have to get sick, Lord. We only know your promise: No matter where we are or what we are called to endure, there you are in the midst of it with us, never leaving our side. Not for a split second. Thank you, Lord of all.

When Jesus saw their faith, he said unto the sick of the palsy, Son, thy sins be forgiven thee.

—Mark 2:5

Jesus, the man who was sick of the palsy was carried to you by four friends, who very creatively found a way to lower him from the rooftop. Thank you for those friends who carry me to you in prayer when I am at the end of my rope. Help me to be that friend to others.

But if we hope for that we see not, then do we with patience wait for it.

—Romans 8:25

It is hard to be patient, but I am grateful for that gift. Whether it is waiting in line or anticipating a coming event, patience is a wonderful way to slow down and appreciate what is coming. Thank you for the gift of patience and the ability to take my time and savor every moment. Instead of saying, "I can't wait!" I am happy to say, "I will wait my turn" as I anticipate what is to come.

For which cause we faint not; but though our outward man perish, yet the inward man is renewed day by day.

—2 Corinthians 4:16

Finally, I've emerged from the dark night. Into the light with new energy, renewed vigor, a body that responds again. Thank you for recovery and wholeness. And bless me as I tell others how good you are!

He is thy praise, and he is thy God, that hath done for thee these great and terrible things, which thine eyes have seen.

—Deuteronomy 10:21

Today I will think about the miracles in my life. I am thankful that God gives me these special gifts. Miracles remind me that God is always in my life. Thank you, Lord, for showing me your power and surprising me with these moments of grace. Help me see your hand at work and trust that your way is the best.

And we have known and believed the love that God hath to us. God is love; and he that dwelleth in love dwelleth in God, and God in him.

—1 John 4:16

Father, thank you for initiating our wonderful relationship by loving me first! Your perfect love has taught me to trust you and leave my fear of your judgment behind. Your love for me brings such joy to my life, Lord. Help me spread this joy to others today.

Keep thy heart with all diligence; for out of it are the issues of life.

—Proverbs 4:23

Lord, many times I have asked you to protect my heart from wanton wanderings, and you have always aided me. How grateful I am for your help, Lord. Thank you for steering my heart toward only what is good and true. My heart is full of love for many people, but it only belongs to you.

February

God is able to make all grace abound toward you; that ye, always having all sufficiency in all things, may abound to every good work.

—2 Corinthians 9:8

Well, it's a new month. We're in the dregs of winter, though, and it's hard to feel fresh and new. It's been gray and dreary outside, and the kids are bored and restless, tired of school and eager for spring sports to begin again.

Lord, I know you take us where we're at. Please give me the grace to see the blessings in the ordinary and humdrum. Thank you for the crises that aren't happening, the text from a friend with a funny joke, my spouse taking the car in for an oil change. Bless my family, and my friends, and the service workers I meet as I run my errands.

I have rejoiced in the way of thy testimonies, as much as in all riches.

—Psalm 119:14

Thank you, Father, for your Holy Spirit, who guides me through each day. May I willingly follow his lead, no matter when or where. Help me to obey quickly when he directs me to serve or forgive others. May I always be thankful and rejoice in the blessings he points out to me along the way.

God hath set some in the church, first apostles, secondarily prophets, thirdly teachers, after that miracles, then gifts of healings, helps, governments, diversities of tongues.

—1 Corinthians 12:28

Lord, in your infinite wisdom you knew we would need instruction for life, and so you placed in your Word the guidelines for living a productive life that brings you glory. Your Word nurtures us body and soul and keeps our minds focused on the beautiful, positive aspects of life. Thank you, Lord, for not leaving us here without a guidebook. We'd be lost without your Word.

He restoreth my soul: he leadeth me in the paths
of righteousness for his name's sake.

—Psalm 23:3

How can I rejoice when I'm having "one of those
days," Father? How can I pray continually when I
feel overwhelmed?

When I look to Jesus' example, I find the answers
I seek. He didn't stay on his knees 24/7, but he
did maintain an ongoing dialogue with you. He
acknowledged that he would prefer to avoid his
cross, but he willingly took it up because it was
necessary. He focused on the joy to come later, in
due time.

I too can give thanks for the good things in my life,
even when bad things are bearing down on me. I
can keep up a dialogue with you as I go about my
day, and I can be joyful in a deep abiding sense,
knowing that all is in your hands.

I know thy works: behold, I have set before thee an open door, and no man can shut it: for thou hast a little strength, and hast kept my word, and hast not denied my name.

—Revelation 3:8

An open door is an invitation. Just as the gates of Heaven are open to all who follow God's will, an open door invites me in to experience new joys and revelations. Thank you, God, for allowing me to see the open doors in my life and take advantage of new experiences. Let me walk through them with Jesus at my side.

Every good gift and every perfect gift is from above, and cometh down from the Father of lights, with whom is no variableness, neither shadow of turning.

—James 1:17

To embrace the gifts each day brings is to acknowledge that the Creator never walks away from his creation. Rather, his hand is always at work making us better than we know we can be.

A new commandment I give unto you, That ye love one another; as I have loved you, that ye also love one another.

—John 13:34

God,

Teach me to walk in love today. With the stressful and hectic nature of life, I find myself giving in to anger, unkindness, and even hatred, and that is not how I want to live or behave. Help me turn to a loving solution for every problem, and to stand in love even when I am surrounded by negativity and confusion. Show me how to always depend on your love, even if at times my own capacity to love others fails me. I ask that I always try to be a loving channel of your presence, and that in the times when I am failing, you come to my aid and remind me of the precious power of love and how much it is needed in this world. Thank you, God. Amen.

A friend loveth at all times, and a brother is born for adversity.

—Proverbs 17:17

Thank you, God, for those in my life who are like family... the childhood friend who has become a sister of the heart, the college friend who has been an honorary uncle to the kids, the neighbor who dispenses grandfatherly wisdom. Thank you for the blessing of love. Let me, too, open my heart to others.

Two are better than one; because they have a good reward for their labour.

—Ecclesiastes 4:9

Terri's elderly mom, who has been struggling to keep up her house, is preparing the home for sale, and Terri offered to help with yard work. After one day of working the large, overgrown property, Terri confessed to a friend that she was feeling overwhelmed. Her friend not only offered to help, but showed up with her two cheerful sons in tow. "Working together, we had the yard in shape within a day!" Terri enthused. "It was fun!"

Dear Lord, you put friends in my life, and I thank you; working together, my friends and I can move mountains. Many together can accomplish much, and there is joy in the sharing!

For all things are for your sakes, that the abundant grace might through the thanksgiving of many redound to the glory of God.

—2 Corinthians 4:15

As we learn to trust you, God, we discover your strengthening presence in various places and people. Wherever we encounter shelter, comfort, rest, and peace, we are bound to hear your voice, welcoming us. And in whomever we find truth, love, gentleness, and humility, we are sure to hear your heartbeat, assuring us that you will always be near. Thank you, God. Amen.

Who now rejoice in my sufferings for you, and fill up that which is behind of the afflictions of Christ in my flesh for his body's sake, which is the church.

—Colossians 1:24

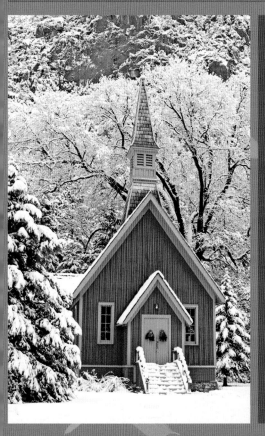

Lord, you do not leave us to suffer alone. You are with us in pain, in sickness, and in our worst moments. Thank you for your comfort and healing power. Thank you for getting us through when our bodies fail, when our health falters, and when we need you most of all. Amen.

I say therefore to the unmarried and widows, it is good for them if they abide even as I.

—1 Corinthians 7:8

My God, I thank you for the blessings of the single life.

One of your plans was for people to get married and have children. But I know that your good and perfect will is also for some of us to live unmarried and not have children.

For this life I thank you. For the gift to be free to learn to love without clinging. To seek relationships without owning, to offer my love and kindness among many friends.

Yes, Lord, at times I am lonely, like all people can be. So I ask you to fill those times of emptiness with your presence. Enter into the barren places with your refreshing water of life.

And as I continue on this path—living by myself—keep my friends and family close, no matter how far away they live. Give me peace in my daily work, joy in the pursuit of wholeness, and comfort in the solitary nights. And please continue to give me a giving heart. For I know, Lord, I am blessed.

I will praise thee; for I am fearfully and wonderfully made: marvellous are thy works; and that my soul knoweth right well.

—Psalm 139:14

Today I am going to treat myself! Thank you for the opportunity to do something special "just because." Thank you for giving me the chance to reward myself just for being me. I am grateful for these little joys and for the ability to recognize that I am worthy of pampering. My life is special, and today I am thankful for the chance to rejoice in myself.

Beloved, let us love one another: for love is of God; and every one that loveth is born of God, and knoweth God. He that loveth not knoweth not God; for God is love.

—1 John 4:7–8

It's Valentine's Day! While this holiday can be commercial, let me take it as an opportunity to thank you, God, for the people I love and the people who love me. I know all love ultimately flows from you, for you are love.

My son, eat thou honey, because it is good; and the honeycomb, which is sweet to thy taste.

—Proverbs 24:13

How grateful I am for the sweet things I eat! Of course, I don't want to overindulge, but I get so much enjoyment out of the sweet taste! Thank you, God, for creating sweet foods. Help me enjoy them in moderation and always praise you for the sweetness in my life.

For where your treasure is, there will your heart be also.

—Matthew 6:21

Lord, my heart is uplifted as I think of the special gift you have given me: a community of faith. I thank you for my church and for the dear people who have become part of my support system. I thank you for your invitation to spend time with you.

My husband and children and I need the blessings of church attendance. We need the fellowship and care of other believers; we need to be refreshed with the words of Scripture and feel the power of prayer washing over us. We need to experience your presence, Lord, in your house, and to become involved in your work.

Please continue to strengthen our children's ties to your church so that they, too, may participate in the joys of life in the Christian community.

I beseech you therefore, brethren, by the mercies of God, that ye present your bodies a living sacrifice, holy, acceptable unto God, which is your reasonable service.

—Romans 12:1

Thank you for the gift of ancestral faith. May I, as I take my place in the family portrait as the next generation, continue to keep you, everlasting God, as the centerpiece of our family, for your love is as ageless and steadfast as the wind calling my name. Watch over the grandchildren as you have over me in your special ways. Listen as I call out their names in echoes of those family prayers shared on my behalf through a lifetime of faith-full love.

Lo, children are an heritage of the Lord; and the fruit of the womb is his reward.

—Psalm 127:3

How can I thank you enough for my spouse and children? When I step back from everyday concerns for a moment, I am overwhelmed with appreciation. We all have our flaws and sins, but you've given us a home full of love for each other. Please protect us from harm, guide us in your paths towards wisdom, and bless us abundantly.

For every house is builded by some man; but he that built all things is God.

—Hebrews 3:4

I am so grateful for my home! It may not be fancy, but it is my own place. How lucky I am to have a place to live safely. How good it is sometimes to retreat from the world and be alone with my things, my routines, and my space. Thank you, Lord, for giving me shelter and a place to call my own.

If thou wilt make me an altar of stone, thou shalt not build it of hewn stone: for if thou lift up thy tool upon it, thou hast polluted it.

—Exodus 20:25

How glad I am that we have tools to help us work! Even a tool as simple as a hammer or a screwdriver can make a job easier. Thank you, Lord, for giving us the tools we need to do our jobs. Help us to be tools as well and to make others lives easier through our assistance.

Let the beauty of the Lord our God be upon us:
and establish thou the work of our hands upon us;
yea, the work of our hands establish thou it.

—Psalm 90:17

Today I am tired, Lord. There seem to be too many
things on my to-do list and too few hours in the
day. And still, I know what a blessing it is to have
work to do and to live a purpose-filled life. Thank
you for tasks large and small that give meaning to
our days, Lord. May we always do each one as if
we were doing it only for you. And may we never
assume we can do anything without your direction
and energy.

> Now the God of patience and consolation grant you to be likeminded one toward another according to Christ Jesus.
>
> —Romans 15:5

Dear God,

It's been difficult lately. One challenge after another, one obstacle after the next. But I know everything is for my greatest growth and to teach me valuable lessons, and for that I come to you today to give thanks and praise. I may get angry and frustrated when life gets derailed, but I know in my heart you are never giving me more than I can handle, and that there is a blessing on the other side of each lesson you provide me with. Those blessings are what keep me going, even on the most troubling of days. Thank you for caring about me enough to push me and motivate me to grow, to become a stronger, better person through my trials and tribulations. I truly am blessed. Amen.

I will walk among you, and will be your God, and ye shall be my people.

—Leviticus 26:12

How amazing you are, O Lord! You are all-powerful and all-knowing, and yet you promise to walk with me. You sent Jesus, your son, to live as one of us, to walk among us. You claim us as your own. When I am feeling downcast, let me remember that the Lord of the universe chooses to love me. Thank you and praise you!

Thou shalt love the Lord thy God with all thy heart, and with all thy soul, and with all thy mind, and with all thy strength: this is the first commandment.

—Mark 12:30

O Lord, your gift of love is often distorted in this world of ours. You are the source of the only perfect love we will ever know. Thank you, Lord, for abiding in us and helping us love ourselves and others. On this day, Lord, I pray that you will draw near to anyone who is feeling unloved. May they accept your unconditional love so they will know what true love is!

The mighty God, even the Lord, hath spoken, and called the earth from the rising of the sun unto the going down thereof.

—Psalm 50:1

Slowly but surely, the days are getting longer again. I'm impatient for spring to arrive. But before it does... I thank you for the blessings of the winter, God. The holidays, the snow days, the celebration of your birth. I thank you for warm clothes and hot chocolate, and the days the car started despite the chill. I thank you even for bare tree branches and gray slush!

And as the days get longer, let me appreciate the extra sunlight as a gift, a daily grace that reminds me of your love.

He that getteth wisdom loveth his own soul: he that keepeth understanding shall find good.

—Proverbs 19:8

Lord, you come to us in the storm, the fire, and even in the stillness of a quiet moment. Sometimes your message is strong, carried on bustling angelic wings; sometimes our spirits are nudged, our hearts lightened by the gentle whisper of spirit voices. However you approach us, your message is always one of tender love and compassion. Thank you for the certainty—and the surprise—of your holy voice.

He, that being often reproved hardeneth his neck, shall suddenly be destroyed, and that without remedy.

—Proverbs 29:1

God, help me to accept the help I need and to give up my stubborn need to control the outcome of every situation. Show me that sometimes my will is not always the best and that sometimes you send us healing angels in the form of other humans. Thank you. Amen.

Come now, and let us reason together, saith the Lord: though your sins be as scarlet, they shall be as white as snow; though they be red like crimson, they shall be as wool.

—Isaiah 1:18

On laundry day, as I'm removing stains that have been allowed to set, I remember this verse. Thank you for the power of your forgiveness. Please let me turn to you in repentance as soon as I've done something wrong, not allowing that sin to set and deepen and become habitual.

Open thou mine eyes, that I may behold wondrous things out of thy law.

—Psalm 119:18

Lord, thank you for this Leap Day! Let me treat this not just as any other day, but as a special gift, a chance to turn to anew. I ask that you open my eyes today to all the instances of grace around me. Let me take a special delight in the splendor of your creation. Let me see the best in people today. Let me see even the people who get my back up with your eyes, the eyes of love.

March

And Jesus being full of the Holy Ghost returned from Jordan, and was led by the Spirit into the wilderness.

—Luke 4:1

Thank you, God, for this new month. This month brings the first inklings of spring to my area, though the trees are still bare. But that seems appropriate, during this month that takes place during the season of Lent. Lord, this month, empty my heart of distractions. Walk with me to the desert and stay with me there, as you pare away those things that draw me away from you.

Let us come before his presence with thanksgiving, and make a joyful noise unto him with psalms.

—Psalm 95:2

Even when you feel like you have nothing, the love of God remains. Being thankful for his presence will open your eyes to what you do have, and maybe never noticed before. God is always showering you with reasons to be thankful. Even when you feel like all is lost, God is there, and that alone is something to be grateful for.

I have called upon thee, for thou wilt hear me, O God: incline thine ear unto me, and hear my speech.

—Psalm 17:6

How good it is to talk to God! Formal prayer is important, but today I just want to pour out my heart and speak to God in my own words. Thank you for the opportunity to talk to you as a friend. Thank you for listening to my prayers and understanding my heart.

Bear ye one another's burdens, and so fulfil the law of Christ.

—Galatians 6:2

Thank you, Lord, for helping us through our hard times. You have shown your love for us and made us more compassionate people. Help us show the same love to others who are going through hard times.

But whoso hath this world's good, and seeth his brother have need, and shutteth up his bowels of compassion from him, how dwelleth the love of God in him?

—1 John 3:17

Renee's grandmother would say, "Welcome challenging times, and see who your friends are." Renee experienced that first hand when she became caregiver for her ailing dad. Over time, she learned who thought of her friendship as a priority: some relationships faded because Renee's schedule was no longer as flexible. It was painful to realize that not all her friendships were as close as she'd thought, but looking back now, she appreciates—and celebrates—the friends who stuck by her.

God, thank you for those friends who love and support us through hard times.

Heal me, O Lord, and I shall be healed; save me, and I shall be saved: for thou art my praise.

—Jeremiah 17:14

Creator God, you have come to me with healing in your hand. When I cried out, you heard me. You provided me with a gift that brought both peace and pleasure to my harried life. You helped me to focus on life instead of illness and sorrow. Lord, thank you for this wondrous gift. Amen.

What? know ye not that your body is the temple of the Holy Ghost which is in you, which ye have of God, and ye are not your own? For ye are bought with a price: therefore glorify God in your body, and in your spirit, which are God's.

—1 Corinthians 6:19-20

Father, this morning I woke up, and the gift of life was still within me. What a privilege! I don't want to lose wonder of it for even one day. So help me to live with purpose and joy, not waiting for what today might bring me, but rather looking for opportunities to be and do all that you've created me for. And, most of all, thank you for being with me in each moment, showing me the way of abundant living.

Ye shall not fear them: for the Lord your God he shall fight for you.

—Deuteronomy 3:22

When sixteen-year-old Kate auditioned for the school play, she was surprised to be cast in a substantial role. She loved rehearsals and connected with fellow cast members, but as the date of the show approached, she found herself increasingly consumed with doubt. What if she froze on stage? She wished she could drop out of the play, but her dad encouraged her to pray for courage. She did so. "I'm so glad I stuck with it," Kate says now.

God, I know it's okay to have stage fright, but I mustn't let fear stop me. Thank you for helping me work through my fears.

But thou, O Lord, art a God full of compassion, and gracious, long suffering, and plenteous in mercy and truth.

—Psalm 86:15

Thank you, Lord, for reaching out and drawing me under your wings. Even though I am just one of billions of people who need you, your love is so great that you know my troubles, are concerned for my welfare, and are working to renew my dreams. I am so blessed to have you to turn to when I am faced with a calamity, and I am so very grateful that I have you to lean on. I praise you with all my heart. Amen.

The heavens declare the glory of God; and the firmament sheweth his handywork.

—Psalm 19:1

Winters can be long, Lord, as I've complained before, and hope elusive. Thank you for sending me outdoors. My spirit soars at the sight of a woodchuck waking from winter sleep. I rub sleep from my eyes, grateful for signposts of change, like pawprints in the mud, leading me to springs of the soul.

The wind bloweth where it listeth, and thou hearest the sound thereof, but canst not tell whence it cometh, and whither it goeth: so is every one that is born of the Spirit.

—John 3:8

Listen to the wind! I am thankful for its power. The wind is a gift that freshens the air and scrubs it clean. Without the wind, our weather would never change. Thank you, God, for the blessing of the wind and the power it has to change our world and make all things fresh and new.

He giveth power to the faint; and to them that have no might he increaseth strength.

—Isaiah 40:29

Lord, just when I was thinking I was too pooped to get through the day, I heard a praise song on the radio. It reminded me of the unending supply of energy and strength that is ours through faith in you! Thanks for getting me through the day today, Lord. I would be so lost without you.

Speaking to yourselves in psalms and hymns and spiritual songs, singing and making melody in your heart to the Lord.

—Ephesians 5:19

Music fills my heart today! I am so grateful for music in all its forms: the loud thump of rock music, the pretty complexities of a classical symphony, the simple melody of a whistled tune. Thank you, God, for putting music into the world and letting it fill my heart with emotion.

Finally, brethren, whatsoever things are true, whatsoever things are honest, whatsoever things are just, whatsoever things are pure, whatsoever things are lovely, whatsoever things are of good report; if there be any virtue, and if there be any praise, think on these things.

—Philippians 4:8

Thank you, Lord, for the hobbies that I enjoy. How much joy I get out of these pleasures! Thank you for the chance to create, play, and enjoy. I am grateful for the people who share my hobby and who have become my friends. What a gift to share the joy of our pastimes together!

As every man hath received the gift, even so minister the same one to another, as good stewards of the manifold grace of God.

—1 Peter 4:10

Thank you, Lord, for the inner light that shines within me. Help me to show that light to others and not hide it deep inside myself. Thank you for my talents and the things that I am good at. May I never forget how grateful I am to be able to share my abilities and bring joy to others.

The Lord lift up
his countenance
upon thee, and
give thee peace.

—Numbers 6:26

Walking through the neighborhood on a sunny day,
I exchanged smiles with an elderly couple doing
the same. Thank you for this moment of shared
joy. Sometimes your gifts are big ones. Sometimes
they're small and simple: a sunny day, the rustling of
the trees, a smile from a stranger, a sense of peace.

That is, that I may be comforted together with you by the mutual faith both of you and me.

—Romans 1:12

Sharon has been participating in a morning exercise class for three years; the class gets her day off to a good start. A few weeks ago she was surprised when a classmate, a woman she hardly knows, approached her after the morning session and thanked her for always maintaining an attitude of positivity. "She said my cheerfulness uplifts her," Sharon remembers. "I was gratified—and humbled to realize that how I act can affect even those I barely know."

You never know whom you might inspire through your actions. Dear God, may I live a life of faith, cheer, and humility; help me to live in a way that uplifts others.

She is like the merchants' ships; she bringeth her food from afar.

—Proverbs 31:14

The recession hit our family hard, but I'm proud of the way my husband and I stepped up and managed what could have been a scary situation. I've worked outside the home since our children were small, but after the market collapse, my husband was laid off and we both took on a series of extra jobs to make ends meet. It wasn't always easy, but together, we have stayed on top of the bills and kept things stable for the kids. I see the same grit in my sister, who is a young widow with a son of her own. "Women are strong," I tell her, and I mean it.

Dear Lord, thank you for this strength. Women are providers!

Wherefore comfort yourselves together, and edify one another, even as also ye do.

—1 Thessalonians 5:11

Thank God for the friends who lift you up when you feel low; they share the weight when your own load is too heavy to bear.

Thank you for each precious day,

For songs we sing and words we say,

For times of prayer and times of play.

Thank you for the sky and sun,

For days with clouds or days with none,

For the peace that comes when each day's done.

Thank you for your Spirit sent

To make straight the paths that have been bent

To watch over us in all events.

The earth is the Lord's, and the fulness thereof; the world, and they that dwell therein.

—Psalm 24:1

The trees are just beginning to bud, and my neighbor's daffodils arc brightening the view. Thank you for spring, God, for new beginnings. I marvel in the beauty of your creation, the intricacies of your designs. I ask that you keep my eyes open to the wonders of nature.

And let the peace of God rule in your hearts, to the which also ye are called in one body; and be ye thankful.

—Colossians 3:15

Thank you for your wise ways, Lord. Following them fills my life with true blessings—the riches of love and relationship, joy and provision, peace and protection. I remember reading in your Word that whenever I ask for your wisdom from a faith-filled heart, you will give it, no holds barred. So I'll ask once again today for your insight and understanding as I build, using your blueprints.

As ye have therefore received Christ Jesus the Lord, so walk ye in him: Rooted and built up in him, and stablished in the faith, as ye have been taught, abounding therein with thanksgiving.

—Colossians 2:6-7

Jesus was the fulfillment of God's promise of salvation. His life and death made salvation possible for us. What a glorious, selfless gift! I ponder this blessing every day, and gratitude and joy fill my very being.

And when Jesus had cried with a loud voice, he said, Father, into thy hands I commend my spirit: and having said thus, he gave up the ghost.

—Luke 23:46

You gave us the incredible gift of your son, Father God. Thank you.

What do I need to put in your hands? What do I need to release to you? With what do I need to trust you?

All glory be to thee, Most High,

to thee all adoration.

In grace and truth thou drawest nigh

to offer us salvation.

Thou showest thy goodwill to men,

and peace shall reign on earth again;

we praise thy name forever.

—Traditional hymn

Now the Lord of peace himself give you peace always by all means. The Lord be with you all.

—2 Thessalonians 3:16

Lord, how grateful we are for the rest you bring to even the most harried souls. The young soldier on the battlefield knows that peace, and so does the young mother with many mouths to feed but too little money in her bank account. You are the one who brings us to the place of restoration in our hearts and minds, Lord. Thank you for being our shepherd.

The God of my rock; in him will I trust: he is my shield, and the horn of my salvation, my high tower, and my refuge, my saviour; thou savest me from violence. I will call on the Lord, who is worthy to be praised: so shall I be saved from mine enemies.

—2 Samuel 22:3-4

We are grateful, O God, for glimpses we are given of you during times like these. Thank you for showing us how, during raging winds, the mother cardinal refuses to move, standing like a mighty shelter over the fledglings beneath her wings. Secure us in the truth that we, the children of your heart, are likewise watched over and protected during life's storms.

The Lord is my shepherd; I shall not want.

He maketh me to lie down in green pastures: he leadeth me beside the still waters.

He restoreth my soul: he leadeth me in the paths of righteousness for his name's sake.

Yea, though I walk through the valley of the shadow of death, I will fear no evil: for thou art with me; thy rod and thy staff they comfort me.

Thou preparest a table before me in the presence of mine enemies: thou anointest my head with oil; my cup runneth over.

Surely goodness and mercy shall follow me all the days of my life: and I will dwell in the house of the Lord for ever.

—Psalm 23:1-6

Lord, when I am sad, you give me hope. When I am lost, you offer me direction and guidance. When I am alone, you stand beside me. When my heart aches with sorrow, you bring me new blessings. Thank you for your gifts of grace, of love, and of healing.

O taste and see that the Lord is good: blessed is the man that trusteth in him.

—Psalm 34:8

Thank you, God, for my five senses. I am grateful for being able to see, hear, taste, touch, and smell. How wonderful to see nature's beauty, to hear the voices of my loved ones, to taste good food, to smell the fresh scent of spring, and to touch a loved one's skin. My senses let me experience the world, and I give thanks for that gift today.

> We walk by faith, not by sight.
>
> —2 Corinthians 5:7

Human faith lives between two extremes, Lord: It's neither completely blind nor able to see everything. It has plenty of evidence when it steps out and trusts you, but it takes each step with a good many questions still unanswered. It's really quite an adventure, this life of faith. And Lord, I must confess that experiencing your faithfulness over time makes it easier and easier to trust you with the unknown in life. Thank you for your unshakable devotion.

Behold, what manner of love the Father hath bestowed upon us, that we should be called the sons of God: therefore the world knoweth us not, because it knew him not.

—1 John 3:1

Precious Lord, fostering kindness in children isn't easy because they are so centered on their own wants and needs. But Lord, I praise you for signs of kindness I have seen in my children. As they grow, I see more evidence of their reaching out to others, and I am thankful.

In your tender mercy, you have allowed some of your goodness to shine through to my children.

Continue to develop in their hearts a compassion for the poor, the ill, the unfortunate, the outcast, so each day they may grow more like you.

April

He fill thy mouth with laughing, and thy lips with rejoicing.

—Job 8:21

Today I am thankful for the gift of laughter. How wonderful it is to let out a big belly laugh and feel joy rush through my entire body! Thank you for the people who make me laugh, whether it is a neighbor or friend or a performer on television. Thank you for allowing me to experience joy bursting out of me, and help me make others feel happy with my laughter as well.

April 2

Therefore will I offer in his tabernacle sacrifices of joy; I will sing, yea, I will sing praises unto the Lord.

—Psalm 27:6

Today I want to praise your name, God. I want to be joyful in a way that spills over, full of awe and thanksgiving. I want to make a sacrifice of praise, to revel in the works of your hands, to delight in your awesome power.

Thou, even thou, art Lord alone; thou hast made heaven, the heaven of heavens, with all their host, the earth, and all things that are therein, the seas, and all that is therein, and thou preservest them all; and the host of heaven worshippeth thee.

—Nehemiah 9:6

Today I take joy in nature. I look around and see all that you have made. The natural world is full of your presence. Thank you for the birds migrating overhead, for the wind's breath, even for the violence of a thunderstorm. I know that everything came to be by your hand, and the world around me is a blessing in my life.

He sendeth the springs into the valleys, which run among the hills.

—Psalm 104:10

The older I get, the more aware I am of the seasons of life, Lord. I know that when we draw our energy and resources from your living Word, we truly can be compared to the trees that thrive near streams of water. The fruit of a young life lived for you may look a bit different than the fruit visible in the lives of older folks, but it all brings you glory. Thank you, Lord, for supplying your living water through all the seasons of our lives. Without it, we could bear no worthy fruit at all.

Then I will give you rain in due season, and the land shall yield her increase, and the trees of the field shall yield their fruit.

—Leviticus 26:4

Thank you for rain! Not only do April showers bring May flowers, as the old saying goes, but rain can be beautiful in its own right. Thank you for gray days and the sound of rain on the rooftop. Thank you when the basement stays dry. Thank you even when a sports event or outdoor party is canceled—when we let those things happen with calm and acceptance, we find out that your plans for us are better than our own.

I do set my bow in the cloud, and it shall be for a token of a covenant between me and the earth.

—Genesis 9:13

Thank you, Lord, for the beauty of a rainbow. What a contrast that peaceful, glowing bow is to the tempest of the storm that came before it! Help me see rainbows as your promise to the world that beauty and happiness can come after pain and brighten my world again.

Be careful for nothing; but in every thing by prayer and supplication with thanksgiving let your requests be made known unto God.

And the peace of God, which passeth all understanding, shall keep your hearts and minds through Christ Jesus.

—Philippians 4:6-7

Dear God, hear my prayer. I am suffering and in need of your merciful blessings. Please take me into your arms. Give me the courage to keep going through difficult times and the fortitude to move beyond the outer illusions of pain and despair. Only you can heal me, God. In praise and thanks, amen.

Put on therefore, as the elect of God, holy and beloved, bowels of mercies, kindness, humbleness of mind, meekness, longsuffering; Forbearing one another, and forgiving one another, if any man have a quarrel against any: even as Christ forgave you, so also do ye. And above all these things put on charity, which is the bond of perfectness.

—Colossians 3:12-14

I thank you for the healing power of friends and for the positive emotions friendship brings. Thank you for sending companions to me so we can support and encourage one another and share our joys and sorrows. My friends represent for me your presence and friendship here on earth. Please keep them in your care, Father. We need each other, and we need you. Amen.

Take heed therefore unto yourselves, and to all the flock, over the which the Holy Ghost hath made you overseers, to feed the church of God, which he hath purchased with his own blood.

—Acts 20:28

Lord, I thank you today for the full community of believers. We are not alone in seeking you out, and in worshipping you. Being around other people of faith can renew my own. I pray today for all that call out to you. May our faith flourish.

And the Word was made flesh, and dwelt among us, (and we beheld his glory, the glory as of the only begotten of the Father,) full of grace and truth.

—John 1:14

Son of God, who came to Earth,

thank you for your love for us.

Son of Man, who dwelt among us,

thank you for your love for us.

Savior, who redeemed the world,

thank you for your love for us.

Jesus, living Word of God,

thank you for your love for us.

For to be carnally minded is death; but to be spiritually minded is life and peace.

—Romans 8:6

Spiritual birth is amazing, Father! It's a miracle no less exciting than the birth of a baby. Your Word says that it causes even the angels in heaven to rejoice. Thank you for my own spiritual birth. It's the reason I'm praying right now and enjoying this fellowship with you. It's so good to be your child. Today I'll just bask in that reality.

But we see Jesus, who was made a little lower than the angels for the suffering of death, crowned with glory and honour; that he by the grace of God should taste death for every man.

—Hebrews 2:9

Jesus, how can we express our gratitude, that you died to save us all? How else but by saying to the Father, as you did in the Garden, "nevertheless not what I will, but what thou wilt" (Mark 14:36).

For God so loved the world, that he gave his only begotten Son, that whosoever believeth in him should not perish, but have everlasting life.

—John 3:16

Dear God, your love embraces me like the warmth of the sun, and I am filled with light. Your hope enfolds me in arms so strong, I lack for nothing. Your grace fills me with the strength I need to move through this day. For these gifts you give me, of eternal love, eternal peace, and most of all, for eternal friendship, I thank you God.

He healeth the broken in heart, and bindeth up
their wounds.

—Psalm 147:3

Thank you, Lord, for enduring unimaginable pain,
even to the point of death, so that my broken
relationship with my heavenly Father can be healed.
By that healing, may all my emotional wounds be
healed as well. In your name, I pray. Amen.

But a certain Samaritan, as he journeyed, came where he was: and when he saw him, he had compassion on him, And went to him, and bound up his wounds, pouring in oil and wine, and set him on his own beast, and brought him to an inn, and took care of him.

—Luke 10:33-34

Father God, thank you for those angelic persons who bring healing. We will try to mimic their ways.

Bless the Lord, ye his angels, that excel in strength, that do his commandments, hearkening unto the voice of his word.

—Psalm 103:20

Father, the wind rustling the leaves reminds me of angel wings all around me. Thank you for such a reminder. Help me stay mindful that the work of angels goes on all the time all around me whether I am aware or not, and that life is even more than I see.

For which cause we faint not; but though our outward man perish, yet the inward man is renewed day by day.

—2 Corinthians 4:16

Lord, today I ask your special blessing on the elderly among us. No matter how old we are, we notice our bodies aging. How difficult it must be to be near the end of life and struggling to hold on to mobility, vision, hearing, and wellness of being. Give us compassion for those older than we are, Lord, and thank you for your promise that you will be with us to the very end of our days.

April 18

The memory of the just is blessed: but the name of the wicked shall rot.

—Proverbs 10:7

Thank you for the gift of memory. Playing "I remember" is such fun, Lord of history, especially the sharing of it with grandchildren who, like relay runners, are here to pick up their part of our family tale.

But if any provide not for his own, and specially for those of his own house, he hath denied the faith, and is worse than an infidel.

—1 Timothy 5:8

Lord, what compassion you showered on your people when you grouped us into families! Thank you, Lord, for the homes we are privileged to enjoy. We are thankful for these sanctuaries for our children and grandchildren. May our homes and our families honor you, Lord, in all we say and do within them. Dwell with us, Lord. You are always welcome.

But Jesus said, Suffer little children, and forbid them not, to come unto me: for of such is the kingdom of heaven.

—Matthew 19:14

Dear God, thank you for children who teach us to be open and forgiving. Help us forgive those who hurt us so the pain will not be passed on through the generations. Thank you for forgiving our sins and help us be at peace with our families. Amen.

Then said Jesus, Father, forgive them; for they
know not what they do.

—Luke 23:34

Even on the cross, Jesus, you extended
forgiveness and understanding. Thank you for this
awesome gift.

> Give me understanding, and I shall keep thy law;
> yea, I shall observe it with my whole heart.
>
> —Psalm 119:34

Lord,

I know that I am only human, and not meant to understand your mysterious ways. To me, life sometimes makes no sense, and things happen I just can't wrap my mind around. Please help me have a sense of peace, a sense of understanding that it all does make sense, and that everything happens for a reason, even if you are the only one who knows what that reason is. Help me feel more balance, harmony, and serenity even when I'm afraid and uncertain. Your love alone can make me feel as though everything is just the way it was meant to be, and that my life does have purpose and meaning. Thank you, Lord. Amen.

That he would grant you, according to the riches of his glory, to be strengthened with might by his Spirit in the inner man; That Christ may dwell in your hearts by faith.

—Ephesians 3:16-17

God, thank you for letting me cling to the faith that has sustained me through so much uncertainty and pain before. I now know that although faith may be all I have, it's also all I need.

Let thy tender mercies come unto me, that I may live: for thy law is my delight.

—Psalm 119:77

Heavenly Father, it is good to remember that everything that lives and breathes is sacred to you. We must never feel superior to any other human being—for we are all precious in your eyes. You have given us life, and we must make the choices that lead to kindness and peace. You created us, but how we live together is up to us. Thank you.

Thank you for both rain and sun.

Thank you for both night and day.

Thank you for both quiet and noise.

Thank you for both challenges and peaceful times.

Thank you when I have little, and thank you when I have much.

Thank you in all times.

For I was an hungred, and ye gave me meat: I was thirsty, and ye gave me drink: I was a stranger, and ye took me in: Naked, and ye clothed me: I was sick, and ye visited me: I was in prison, and ye came unto me.

—Matthew 25:35-36

When I don't feel well, it is easy to feel sorry for myself. Then I remember the people who support me and help me when I am unwell. Thank you for the friends and family, the neighbors and coworkers, the nurses and doctors, and everyone else who goes out of the way to brighten my day and make me see a ray of light in the darkness.

Now I beseech you, brethren, by the name of our Lord Jesus Christ, that ye all speak the same thing, and that there be no divisions among you; but that ye be perfectly joined together in the same mind and in the same judgment.

—1 Corinthians 1:10

It is good, dear God, to be a part of this family: circle of love, place of rest, bastion of peace. When every other source of comfort fails, this is where I return. Thank you for being in our midst.

And God created great whales, and every living creature that moveth, which the waters brought forth abundantly, after their kind, and every winged fowl after his kind: and God saw that it was good.

—Genesis 1:21

Lord, thank you for these angels who come to me in fluff and fur. Thank you for their magic of putting laughter in the hearts of those they love. Thanks for their trust and their unabashed desire to give affection and to be scratched behind the ears.

I thank my God always on your behalf, for the grace of God which is given you by Jesus Christ.

—1 Corinthians 1:4

Gracious and healing God, thank you for everything you have done for me in the past.

You have restored me in unexpected ways and I will never be the same.

Thank you for being with me in the present and for the bright future you have planned for me. I pray for those who don't know you yet, who don't understand how you bless them again and again.

Use me to share the gratitude I feel, that others may grow to know you and your power.

In the name of Jesus, who healed the sick and made the lame to walk, I pray.

Amen.

All people that on earth do dwell,
sing to the Lord with cheerful voice.
Serve him with joy, his praises tell,
come now before him and rejoice!

Know that the Lord is God indeed;
he formed us all without our aid.
We are the flock he comes to feed,
the sheep who by his hand were made.

O enter then his gates with joy,
within his courts his praise proclaim.
Let thankful songs your tongues employ.
O bless and magnify his name.

Trust that the Lord our God is good,
his mercy is forever sure.
His faithfulness at all times stood
and shall from age to age endure.
—William Kethe

May

Give thanks unto the Lord, call upon his name, make known his deeds among the people.

—1 Chronicles 16:8

Have you ever been overwhelmed with gratitude toward God? Ever started singing a favorite hymn or worship song just because you wanted to let God know how much you love him? That's the work of God's Spirit in us, filling us with praise, thanks, and love. These are precious offerings held in God's treasury of remembrance, just as we hold our own children's love gifts close to our hearts. Perhaps there is a love gift you would care to offer your heavenly Father even now as you consider his goodness.

Who knoweth not in all these that the hand of the Lord had wrought this? In whose hand is the soul of every living thing, and the breath of all mankind.

—Job 12:9-10

It's amazing how much joy an animal can bring into our lives. Today I am thankful for my pets— the ones I've had and the ones I know now. I am grateful for their love and companionship, and for somehow knowing when I need a hug or a cuddle. Sometimes it is good to just talk to animals and feel like they are really listening. Thank you, Lord, for the gift of animal companions.

The flowers appear on the earth; the time of the singing of birds is come, and the voice of the turtle is heard in our land.

—Song of Solomon 2:12

Taking an evening walk around my neighborhood, I pass both beautifully cultivated gardens with colorful roses and the edges of a forest preserve, where small, bright wildflowers peep from the brush. I thank you for the beauty that both of them bring into the world. Your creations are wonderful, Lord!

Know ye not that ye are the temple of God, and that the Spirit of God dwelleth in you? If any man defile the temple of God, him shall God destroy; for the temple of God is holy, which temple ye are.

—1 Corinthians 3:16-17

Lord, how hopelessly aware we are of our earthly bodies. They develop creaks and frailties—not to mention weird bumps and lumps! But thanks to you, we are so much more than our bodies. For although we live in the flesh, we are filled with your Holy Spirit; the life we live is really you living out your life in us! Thank you for that perspective, Lord. It makes it so much easier to watch our earthly bodies begin to fail. How ready we will be to exchange them for the heavenly models!

For the word of God is quick, and powerful, and sharper than any twoedged sword, piercing even to the dividing asunder of soul and spirit, and of the joints and marrow, and is a discerner of the thoughts and intents of the heart.

—Hebrews 4:12

Regardless of what the future holds, I'm savoring all sorts of wondrous things I've been too busy to notice before. A thousand daily marvels bring a smile to my face. Through your grace, Lord, rather than thinking how sad it is that I missed them before, I'm delighted to be seeing, doing them now. These small wonders energize me, and for that I'm thankful. It's never too late to be a joyful explorer.

Call unto me, and I will answer thee, and show thee great and mighty things, which thou knowest not.

—Jeremiah 33:3

God, I couldn't help noticing all the loveliness you placed in the world today! This morning I witnessed a sunrise that made my heart beat faster. Then, later, I watched a father gently help his child across a busy parking lot; his tenderness was much like yours. While inside a department store, I spied an elderly couple sitting on a bench. I could hear the man cracking jokes; their laughter lifted my spirits. Then early this evening, I walked by a woman tending her flower bed; she took great pleasure in her work, and her garden was breathtaking. Later, I talked with a friend who is helping some needy families; her genuine compassion inspired me. Thank you, Lord, for everything that is beautiful and good in the world.

Let every one of us please his neighbour for his good to edification.

—Romans 15:2

A good neighbor is a blessing! I am so grateful for the neighbors I have known and who have become my friends just by virtue of living close by. Together we have faced problems and shared memories. Thank you, Lord, for giving me good neighbors who will stand beside me and help make all our lives more complete.

As we have therefore opportunity, let us do good unto all men, especially unto them who are of the household of faith.

—Galatians 6:10

O Lord, we give thanks for your presence, which greets us each day in the guise of a friend, a work of nature, or a story from a stranger. We are reminded through these messengers in our times of deepest need that you are indeed watching over us. Lord, we have known you in the love and care of a friend, who envelopes and keeps us company in our despair. When we observe the last morning glory stretching faithfully to receive what warmth is left in the chilly sunshine, we are heartened and inspired to do the same. When we are hesitant to speak up and then read in the newspaper a story of courage and controversy, we find our voice lifted and strengthened by your message in black-and-white type. Lord, we are grateful receivers of all the angelic messages that surround us every day.

My soul, now praise your Maker!

Let all within me bless His name

Who makes you full partaker

Of mercies more than you dare claim.

Forget Him not whose meekness

Still bears with all your sin,

Who heals your ev'ry weakness,

Renews your life within;

Whose grace and care are endless

And saved you through the past;

Who leaves no suff'rer friendless

But rights the wronged at last.

—Johann Poliander, trans. Catherine Winkworth

Every man according as he purposeth in his heart, so let him give; not grudgingly, or of necessity: for God loveth a cheerful giver.

—2 Corinthians 9:7

Pitching in on the caregiving rotation for my elderly aunt was not something I initially perceived as a blessing, but as a gift I was giving to my aunt and my cousin. Still, God, I thank you for this opportunity to grow, to give, and to learn. The work of caregiving can be stressful and emotionally wearing, but I am learning that when I trust in you and let you work through me, I am able to do the work with a generous heart.

The angel came in unto her, and said, Hail, thou that art highly favoured, the Lord is with thee: blessed art thou among women.

—Luke 1:28

Thank you, God, for such a wonderful role model as the mother of Jesus. So often we sanitize her life, forgetting she was a courageous, creative lady who loved with heart and hand and whose example I pledge to follow.

Train up a child in the way he should go: and when he is old, he will not depart from it.

—Proverbs 22:6

One of my kids talked back to me today, God—and you gave me the grace to handle it well! I know this is something I struggle with, teaching and allowing independence while also instilling values of respect. I've brought this to you in prayer so many times. And today it felt like that habit of prayer paid off; I took a breath and was able to be loving in my response. Thank you, Lord.

The Spirit itself beareth witness with our spirit, that we are the children of God.

—Romans 8:16

The noise of my children fills my heart. I rejoice in their laughter and loud voices. Some days I may not appreciate the tumult children bring into my life. Help me to appreciate their moods, even when they are not always bright and happy. Lead me to be grateful for how much fun childhood can be. Thank you for letting me join my children in enjoying this special time.

A merry heart doeth good like a medicine: but a broken spirit drieth the bones.

—Proverbs 17:22

Lord, how we thank you for the gift of laughter! Even in the midst of grief you send those happy memories that make us laugh and bring comfort to our souls. Laughter is so healing, Lord. It's reassuring to see so much evidence of your sense of humor. I feel confident there will be lots of laughter in heaven!

She openeth her mouth with wisdom; and in her tongue is the law of kindness.

—Proverbs 31:26

Thank you, God, that I'm not the same person today as I was even just a few years ago. This new life as a mother writes its changing tale on my heart, face, and mind like growth rings on a tree. May this tree of life continue to grow into the future where I will provide limbs of love from which my children can launch their own lives.

This is the Lord's doing; it is marvellous in our eyes.

—Psalm 118:23

How beautiful is the work of your hands, Lord! I am grateful for the world of nature. How wonderful it is to see the plants and animals you have created. How awesome is your power on the shape of the Earth! Thank you, Lord, for making the landscape and creating so much beauty in the natural world.

With my soul have I desired thee in the night; yea, with my spirit within me will I seek thee early: for when thy judgments are in the earth, the inhabitants of the world will learn righteousness.

—Isaiah 26:9

God, you are so great. It is always the right time to worship you, but morning is best. Praise for the dawning light that streams in through this window. Praise for the sound of the birds as they flit through in the air. Praise for the little spider crawling along on the ceiling. Praise for the smell of coffee and the warmth of a cup in my hands. Praise for the flowering plants—and even those weeds growing by the house. Praise for the neighbors walking along the sidewalk and the clouds moving by, too. Most of all, praise for the breath that keeps flowing in and out of my lungs. Yes, this is the greatest item of praise: that you alone are my life—all life itself. Without you, all is dust. Praise... for you.

The Lord is nigh unto all them that call upon him, to all that call upon him in truth.

—Psalm 145:18

It's hard, Lord, to reveal my heart to you, though it's the thing I most want to do. Remind me in this dialogue that you already know what is within me. You wait—O thank you!—hoping for the gift of my willingness to acknowledge the good you already see and the bad you've long forgotten.

If we confess our sins, he is faithful and just to forgive us our sins, and to cleanse us from all unrighteousness.

—1 John 1:9

I am grateful that you don't require spiritual gymnastics from me when I sin, Lord. You just call me to come to you with a humble and repentant heart. In my pride I sometimes want to do something that will impress you—something that will "make up for it" somehow. But you just shake your head and keep calling me to humble myself and bring my sincere sorrow to you. That often doesn't seem like enough to me. But I guess that's the point: I can never earn your grace; it is a gift. Christ died on the cross for us because it is beyond our powers to make up for all the sins we have committed. I bring my contrite heart before you now, Lord. Thank you for receiving it as an acceptable sacrifice.

If any of you lack wisdom, let him ask of God, that giveth to all men liberally, and upbraideth not; and it shall be given him.

—James 1:5

God, I give thanks for the wisdom you share with me when I am trying to understand my own actions or someone else's. You know what is best, and you have my highest good in mind. I will turn to you for the advice and guidance I need. Thank you, God, for being a strong and loving presence in my life. Amen.

And they which went before rebuked him, that he should hold his peace: but he cried so much the more, Thou son of David, have mercy on me.

—Luke 18:39

The college track was not fruitful or satisfying for Carole, but when she told friends she was thinking of leaving school to start her own business, cutting hair, they discouraged her. "I let myself be convinced that it was foolish to stray from a certain path," Carole says now. It took another difficult school year for her to decide she was ready to strike out on her own. Now she's not only successful in her business, but personally fulfilled.

God, Luke's story of the blind man fills me with hope. Thank you for reminding me that I mustn't let others tell me "what I can't do."

Whatsoever ye do, do it heartily, as to the Lord.

—Colossians 3:23

Thank you for employment. I may not enjoy all aspects of my job, but I'm grateful for the financial security it offers. I'm grateful for the dignity of work, for my conscientious colleagues, and for those days when I feel like I'm getting to use my God-given talents to the full! I ask your blessings today on those looking for employment, that you give them a spirit of hope and patience as they wait for the right work to come along.

For with the heart man believeth unto righteousness; and with the mouth confession is made unto salvation.

—Romans 10:10

Some days the race feels like a sprint, Lord, and on other days, a marathon. I want to press on, but I need you to infuse my spirit with your strength and steadfastness. I want to run and finish well. Thank you for beginning the work of faith in my life and for promising not to stop working until my faith is complete.

Blessed are the merciful: for they shall
obtain mercy.

—Matthew 5:7

For those times when a friend or family members
have forgiven me when I wronged them, I offer
thanks and ask your blessings upon them. They
taught me about how powerful mercy can be. O
merciful God, let me in turn be merciful to others.

May 25

Let brotherly love continue. Be not forgetful to entertain strangers: for thereby some have entertained angels unawares.

—Hebrews 13:1-2

Thank you for those people you have sent in my life who have been angels for me. Let me find ways to be an angel for others.

Seek the Lord and his strength, seek his face continually.

—1 Chronicles 16:11

These hard times help me see with new eyes, Lord. Despite my tears, I see more clearly your tender mercies, my great need for your presence, and the angels in my life I had overlooked or would never have otherwise seen. Thank you for opening my eyes, even as you comfort my heart.

God is our refuge and strength, a very present help in trouble. Therefore will not we fear, though the earth be removed, and though the mountains be carried into the midst of the sea; Though the waters thereof roar and be troubled, though the mountains shake with the swelling thereof.

—Psalm 46:1-3

Teach us to know, God, that it is exactly at the point of our deepest despair that you are closest. For at those times we can finally admit we have wandered in the dark, without a clue. Yet you have been there with us all along. Thank you for your abiding presence.

And ye now therefore have sorrow: but I will see you again, and your heart shall rejoice, and your joy no man taketh from you.

—John 16:22

Dear Lord,

Today I received bad news about something I was so excited about, something I had poured my heart and soul into. I worked so hard on this project and to find out it just won't happen has all but broken my spirit. Thank you for your comfort as I deal with this disappointment, and thank you for helping me to understand the bigger picture behind this. I know that your ways are mysterious, and that you never fail to open a new door when an old one closes, so keep my eyes and my heart focused on the future and the new doors this rejection may lead to. Lift my spirits with your love and faith in me and help me find my enthusiasm and belief in my own abilities again. Thank you, Lord.

Light serene of holy glory

From the Immortal Father poured,

Holy Thou, O blessed Jesus,

Holy, blessed, Christ the Lord.

Now we see the sun descending,

Now declines the evening light,

And in hymns we praise the Father,

Son and Spirit, God of Might.

—Early Christian hymn, trans. John Brownlie

The Lord is my light and my salvation; whom shall I fear? The Lord is the strength of my life; of whom shall I be afraid?

—Psalm 27:1

Lord, you are the light I follow down this long, dark tunnel. You are the voice that whispers, urging me onward when this wall of sorrow seems insurmountable. You are the hand that reaches out and grabs mine when I feel as if I'm sinking in despair. You alone, Lord, are the waters that fill me when I am dried of all hope and faith. I thank you, Lord, for although I may feel like giving up, you have not given up on me. Amen.

What things soever ye desire, when ye pray, believe that ye receive them, and ye shall have them.

—Mark 11:24

Give thanks and praise for what you have, and your prayers are already answered.

June

For by grace are ye saved through faith; and that not of yourselves: it is the gift of God: Not of works, lest any man should boast.

—Ephesians 2:8–9

Father God, you gave a staggering gift through your son, Jesus Christ. How can I express my gratitude for the gift of salvation? Sometimes I need to sit in silence, surrounded by your presence, as I reflect on your love for me.

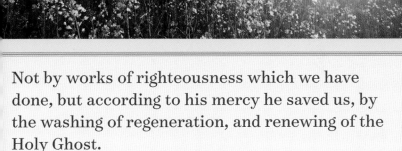

Not by works of righteousness which we have done, but according to his mercy he saved us, by the washing of regeneration, and renewing of the Holy Ghost.

—Titus 3:5

Lord, I am grateful that you don't have a list of criteria for being eligible for salvation. What insecurity that would create in us! I feel blessed that I don't need to resort to servile fear or self-important boasting when it comes to my standing with you. Your salvation is a gift available to all and secured by your merits (not mine). It is received only by grace through faith in you.

I know that thou canst do every thing, and that no thought can be withholden from thee.

—Job 42:2

Sometimes it is so hard to take chances! Thank you, God, for giving me the courage to take a chance and try something new. I am so glad to be able to step out of my comfort zone and find the courage to change. What a gift to know that taking a chance could change my life! Thank you for the excitement of being brave.

All scripture is given by inspiration of God, and is profitable for doctrine, for reproof, for correction, for instruction in righteousness: That the man of God may be perfect, thoroughly furnished unto all good works.

—2 Timothy 3:16-17

You have made things problematic again, Lord, and I need to see that all this upheaval can be a good thing. Help me, Lord. And thank you for showing me that a thoroughly comfortable existence can rob me of real life. In this time of great change, help me, God of tomorrow, tomorrow, and tomorrow, to trust your guiding presence.

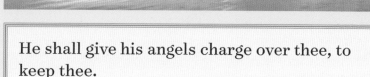

He shall give his angels charge over thee, to keep thee.

—Luke 4:10

Heavenly Father,

We thank you for your holy angels, both those in heaven and those with human names and faces. They make our lives more bearable in times of trouble, and they add to our joy in the good times.

Keep us always in your sight, Lord. When we stumble, please send your merciful messengers to pick us up again. When we are lost, send them to light the way home.

Amen.

Confess your faults one to another, and pray one for another, that ye may be healed. The effectual fervent prayer of a righteous man availeth much.

—James 5:16

Lord, if all the prayers ever prayed were linked together, surely they would reach to heaven and back countless times! We want to be a people who pray without ceasing, Lord. Hear both the prayers we utter and the silent prayers of our hearts, and may you also sense how grateful we are to serve a God who listens to our prayers and sends us his answers.

The Lord will give strength unto his people; the Lord will bless his people with peace.

—Psalm 29:11

It's hard to be grateful for difficult times. Help me to see my trials as an opportunity to grow and change. Help me reach out to others who are suffering their own difficult times. Thank you, God, for the chance to know you better through my suffering. Help me remember and be grateful for the suffering you endured to help me. Let me find the bright side of every trial and the strength to be grateful for the test.

Is any sick among you? let him call for the elders of the church; and let them pray over him, anointing him with oil in the name of the Lord.

—James 5:14

Medicine is such a great gift! I wonder what the wise men and women in olden times would think of the medicines we have today. Thank you, Lord, for giving doctors and scientists the desire and the wisdom to create medicines that help so many people every day. Thank you for their work making my life easier, and for making what was once impossible, very possible today.

By him therefore let us offer the sacrifice of praise to God continually, that is, the fruit of our lips giving thanks to his name.

—Hebrews 13:15

After a routine dental procedure went awry, Megan became very ill. She contracted blood poisoning and the pain in her jaw was beyond anything she'd ever experienced. Thanks to antibiotics and sound medical care, Megan recovered, but now, even months later, when she wakes pain-free she still gives thanks to God. "It took an extreme situation to remind me of the importance of thanking God; being grateful inspires joy, and I feel closer to God than ever," Megan says.

Dear Lord, I understand how important it is to give thanks to you. It draws me closer to you, and is good for my heart.

My God, how endless is your love!
Your gifts are every evening new,
and morning mercies from above
gently distill, like earthly dew.
You spread the curtains of the night,
great Guardian of my sleeping hours;
your sovereign Word restores the light,
and quickens all my drowsy powers.
I yield my powers to your command;
to you I consecrate my days:
perpetual blessings from your hand
demand perpetual songs of praise.
—Isaac Watts

So teach us to number our days, that we may apply our hearts unto wisdom.

—Psalm 90:12

Urge us to pay attention to our need for more time, for it is a worthy yearning. We need all the time we can get. And at the same time, when we find extra hours, restrain us with a gentle hand if we are tempted to squander any of our precious time doing things that seem hardly worth the effort much less worth swapping for a day's pay!

Thank you for the gift of extra time however, whenever, and wherever we gain it. With your guidance, we will be investing it wisely.

For if they fall, the one will lift up his fellow: but woe to him that is alone when he falleth; for he hath not another to help him up.

—Ecclesiastes 4:10

Who guides and protects me in my life? Today, I am grateful for the people who have brought me to where I am today and who always have my best interests at heart. I may not always have appreciated their guidance, but I know deep down they always meant well. In the same way, Lord, let me accept and appreciate your guidance in my life.

For we are labourers together with God: ye are God's husbandry, ye are God's building.

—1 Corinthians 3:9

I look around at work and think how wonderful it is that so many different people can become a team. Thank you, Lord, for my coworkers and supervisors. We may have our differences and our dark moments, but it is good to know that we are all working together toward a common goal. Thank you for the friendships I develop with my coworkers and for bringing us together in a special place.

And they, continuing daily with one accord in the temple, and breaking bread from house to house, did eat their meat with gladness and singleness of heart, Praising God, and having favour with all the people. And the Lord added to the church daily such as should be saved.

—Acts 2:46-47

Thank you for my community. As I run my errands and conduct my business, let me remember to be grateful for everyone who helps me. From a clerk at the store to the police officer keeping me safe, my community is filled with people who help others. Thank you, Lord, for putting these people in my life and for giving me the chance to know them. May I always work to make my community a better place.

Of the Lord ye shall receive the reward of the inheritance: for ye serve the Lord Christ.

—Colossians 3:24

When Noelle first saw the Victorian house that eventually became her home, she knew she had work to do. The house had good bones but had fallen into disrepair, and for months she sanded and painted; her brother even helped her tear out a wall. There were unexpected setbacks. But she prevailed, and now her home is comfortable and a place of refuge. "I thank God," Noelle says. "He gave me the strength to realize my vision."

Dear God, may I always remember to put you at the center of my achievements!

But the salvation of the righteous is of the Lord: he is their strength in the time of trouble.

—Psalm 37:39

You are my strength, my shield, my rock,

my fortress strong against each shock,

my help, my life, my tower,

my battle sword,

almighty Lord—

who can resist your power?

—Adam Reissner, trans. Catherine Winkworth

The Lord is my strength and my shield; my heart trusted in him, and I am helped: therefore my heart greatly rejoiceth; and with my song will I praise him.

—Psalm 28:7

Most merciful God, the helper of all men, so strengthen us by thy power that our sorrow may be turned into joy, and we may continually glorify thy holy name; through Jesus Christ our Lord. Amen.

—11th-century prayer

For ye have not received the spirit of bondage again to fear; but ye have received the Spirit of adoption, whereby we cry, Abba, Father.

—Romans 8:15

Father God, I thank you for your guiding love for me, the love of a father who wants what's best for his child. Your love is the foundation of my life. I thank you for all the gifts you have given me, but most of all, the gift of your love and abiding presence.

If ye then, being evil, know how to give good gifts unto your children: how much more shall your heavenly Father give the Holy Spirit to them that ask him?

—Luke 11:13

Father, thank you for the gift of your Holy Spirit, who guides, protects, and gives solace. I dare to ask that you fill my soul and my life with the gift of your Spirit.

These things have I spoken unto you, that my joy might remain in you, and that your joy might be full.

—John 15:11

Young children have a particularly deep capacity for joy. They love fiercely and play hard; their worldview is often one of opportunity and abundance. As we grow, experiences good and bad accrue. We take on more responsibility, for others and for ourselves, and can lose sight of that deep well of joy. It's still there, if we are mindful. But joy is tricky in that it can manifest itself in opposites: there is joy in community, even as it exists in solitary pursuits. A gorgeous summer sky brings joy, as does a brooding landscape. Sometimes we don't recognize joy, but it is there: we can still access it, whether it feels like good loneliness, hilarity, or a deep stillness. It is a gift we must not lose sight of.

Dear Lord, thank you for the joy which comes from you.

June 21

Now learn a parable of the fig tree. When her branch is yet tender, and putteth forth leaves, ye know that summer is near.

—Mark 13:28

Thank you for the bright colors of summer! I look around and see the sun in the sky, the clear moon in the night, the brilliance of the flowers and the trees. Thank you, Lord, for blessing me with color in my life. I know that even the darkest, dreariest days cannot last forever, just as the memory of winter fades during summer's glory.

For length of days, and long life, and peace, shall they add to thee.

—Proverbs 3:2

May you celebrate this day with all your heart.

Rejoice in the beauty of its light and warmth.

Give thanks for the air and grass and sidewalks.

Let gratitude for other faces flow into your soul.

And cherish the chance to work and play, to think and speak—knowing this:

All simple pleasures are opportunities for praise.

It is not good that the man should be alone; I will make him an help meet for him.

—Genesis 2:18

Thank you, Lord, for our marriage. Like a wedding band, our love encircles but doesn't bind. Like a vow, our love is words but sustains because of what they mean. In your grace, our love has the permanence of rock, not of walls, but of a bridge to moments ahead as special and bright as when we first met.

The Lord God is my strength, and he will make my feet like hinds' feet, and he will make me to walk upon mine high places.

—Habakkuk 3:19

Dear God,

I come to you today giving thanks for all the blessings you've bestowed upon my family. Even through the challenges, your presence has served to remind us we can get through anything with you to lead us. I am forever grateful for the love and grace and mercy you've continued to show us, and for the harder lessons we all have struggled through, and learned from. Knowing we have the love of God to light the way has been the glue that has held us all together. Thank you, God. Amen.

June 25

And God saw every thing that he had made, and, behold, it was very good.

—Genesis 1:31

Thank you today for our pets, past and present! Their uncomplicated affection brings joy to our lives. I ask that you grant them health, long lives, and safety. You made them as you made everything, and I thank you for them!

Who covereth the heaven with clouds, who prepareth rain for the earth, who maketh grass to grow upon the mountains. He giveth to the beast his food, and to the young ravens which cry.

—Psalm 147:8-9

Lord, we praise you for all the beauty and wonder you've placed in the world. How creative of you to think of a creature as exuberant and joyful as the hummingbird! How interesting that you sprinkled spots on the backs of the newborn fawns that follow along behind their mother through our backyard. Let us never become so accustomed to your glorious creation that we take it for granted, Lord. You've blessed us with a wonderland, and we thank you for it.

Now to that God, who has suffered so much for us, who at one giving has conferred on us so many good things, and will yet confer so many more, to this God let every creature who is in heaven or upon the earth, in the sea or in the depth of the abyss, render praise, glory, honor and blessing. He is himself our virtue and our strength. He alone is good, lofty, almighty, admirable, and glorious; the only holy, worthy of praise and blessed through ages of ages. Amen.

—St. Francis of Assisi

The Lord bless thee, and keep thee: The Lord make his face shine upon thee, and be gracious unto thee.

—Numbers 6:24-25

An attitude of gratitude can help you get through even the roughest of times. Focusing on God's blessings helps you realize just how loved you are. It isn't about ignoring all the things that go wrong or bring you suffering, but always remembering to look for the blessing in the lesson, and the silver lining in the dark clouds above.

Let the wicked forsake his way, and the unrighteous man his thoughts: and let him return unto the Lord, and he will have mercy upon him; and to our God, for he will abundantly pardon.

—Isaiah 55:7

I am thankful to the Lord for his gift of forgiveness. I know I am not perfect and I know I make mistakes. Grant me the wisdom and grace to know when I am wrong and to ask for forgiveness. Give me a sense of gratitude toward those who forgive my errors, and help me forgive others who have offended me.

Then came Peter to him, and said, Lord, how oft shall my brother sin against me, and I forgive him? till seven times? Jesus saith unto him, I say not unto thee, Until seven times: but, Until seventy times seven.

—Matthew 18:21-22

Thank you, God, for second chances. Sometimes I feel like I can't do anything right. It's embarrassing to make mistakes. It's embarrassing to show others that I am less than perfect. Thank you for giving me the chance to try again, to make things right, and to improve myself. Help me find the courage to try again and show the world my best qualities!

July

But blessed are your eyes, for they see: and your ears, for they hear.

—Matthew 13:16

God, help me notice the little things and be grateful for them. All too often, we rush through life and don't notice the blessings all around us. I am grateful for the chance to see beauty in the smallest details. Help me remember to slow down and look. I am grateful for the little bits of beauty scattered through my day.

Only by pride cometh contention: but with the well advised is wisdom.

—Proverbs 13:10

Lord, so often I keep doing the same things over and over and getting the same unsatisfying results. This is when I need for you to shine your light on my life and reveal to me all that I haven't been able to see through human eyes. You have all knowledge and every answer to the mysteries of heaven and earth. Show me, Lord. Give me just a bit more of the knowledge you possess. Thank you.

The Lord is not slack concerning his promise, as some men count slackness; but is longsuffering to us-ward, not willing that any should perish, but that all should come to repentance.

—2 Peter 3:9

Thank you, God, for my life. Today I realize I have so much to be thankful for. My life may not be perfect, but nevertheless it is full of good things, of beauty, and of many wonders. Thank you, Lord, for everything you have given me and the opportunities I've had. Please make me aware of all I have to celebrate and be thankful for.

Make a joyful noise unto God, all ye lands.

—Psalm 66:1

Thank you for fireworks! They're a summer sight that I love to see, full of exuberance and creativity. Thank you for the times we have cause to celebrate and gather together to admire and share in this beauty.

And if one prevail against him, two shall withstand him; and a threefold cord is not quickly broken.

—Ecclesiastes 4:12

Dear God, what joy we have in gathering to pray and praise you together. How encouraging it is to share what's happening on our separate life journeys and see your hand at work in so many different ways. Thank you for arranging those times of fellowship, Lord. They are blessed times indeed.

Hatred stirreth up strifes: but love covereth all sins.

—Proverbs 10:12

Thank you for the difficult people in my life. They show me that not everything can be easy. When I try to connect with someone who is hard to get along with or who doesn't agree with me, I think of how Jesus reached out even to those who did not agree with him. Allow me to be like Jesus and be thankful for the opportunity to extend my heart to everyone.

Having then gifts differing according to the grace that is given to us, whether prophecy, let us prophesy according to the proportion of faith; Or ministry, let us wait on our ministering: or he that teacheth, on teaching; Or he that exhorteth, on exhortation: he that giveth, let him do it with simplicity; he that ruleth, with diligence; he that sheweth mercy, with cheerfulness.

—Romans 12:6-8

I am grateful for differences. How boring it would be if every person was the same! How thankful I am not to live in a world full of clones. It's easy to judge others who are different from me, but it is those differences that make the world a wonderful, exciting, and interesting place! Thank you, Lord, for making each person unique and help me to be proud of my own uniqueness.

The stone which the builders refused is become the head stone of the corner.

—Psalm 118:22

How wonderful when God shows us the beauty in something we thought was worthless! I am grateful for the times God opened my eyes to unexpected beauty. Help me to keep my mind open to the wonders all around me and to appreciate everything I see, no matter how insignificant it may seem.

Let your conversation be without covetousness; and be content with such things as ye have: for he hath said, I will never leave thee, nor forsake thee.

—Hebrews 13:5

My husband and I attended a party the other night, and the subject of real estate came up. I love our modest home. We raised our kids there, and we've always been comfortable. But when conversation turned to what makes a house "sell-able," I became embarrassed. We don't have granite countertops in our kitchen, and the bathrooms, while bright, have outdated fixtures. I came home feeling jealous and uneasy: a spirit of materialism briefly made me see our cozy home in a less flattering light. When I woke the next morning, though, refreshed by sleep, my husband and I enjoyed our coffee while watching the birds from our breakfast nook. I looked around our little house and felt joy.

God, you have graced our home with your love. May I not allow materialism to distract me or create anxiety; may I be grateful for the true blessings in my life.

Being enriched in every thing to all bountifulness, which causeth through us thanksgiving to God.

—2 Corinthians 9:11

When I am thankful for what I have, I am given more. When I am not thankful, what I have is taken away. Gratitude is like a door that, when opened, leads to even more good things. But to be ungrateful keeps that door closed, and keeps me away from what God wants to bless me with. I am thankful, always.

In grateful praise, to thee we raise,

Our song today, great God and King;

E'en to the skies, there will arise

The echoes of the songs we sing.

Hallelujah! Hallelujah!

Glory be to God above!

Hallelujah! Hallelujah!

Hallelujah! Hallelujah!

Praise the mighty King, the mighty King,

The King of Love.

We praise thy mighty, great God of right,

We praise thy pow'r and majesty;

We praise thy love, that from above,

Sends down its blessing ceaselessly.

In grateful praise, Lord, all our days,

Our songs shall rise unto the throne;

Grant when, at last, the goal is passed,

We may be gathered with thine own.

—William Henry Gardner

> The Lord shall preserve thy going out and
> thy coming in from this time forth, and even
> for evermore.
>
> —Psalm 121:8

I recently retired after almost 40 years of teaching. As much as I enjoyed my job, I am reveling in the opportunities this new chapter affords. I have always loved travel, and for many years dreamed of visiting Europe; my gift to myself this next year is a month-long tour through France and Italy. While I am excited, I am also a little anxious: I'll be traveling solo, and have never been away from home for so long.

Dear God, thank you for this opportunity. Please bless my travels. Please guide and protect me as I visit new places, meet new people, and broaden my horizons. May I make the most of this journey.

And the Lord, he it is that doth go before thee; he will be with thee, he will not fail thee, neither forsake thee: fear not, neither be dismayed.

—Deuteronomy 31:8

Every day is a journey through time and space. Thank you, Lord, for the journeys that make up my life and take me to amazing places. I am grateful for the things I've learned on my life's journey. Allow me to appreciate the journey more than the destination and keep an open mind for the unexpected gifts on the road. I may not always end up where I thought I would, but I am grateful for the paths I travel!

All things were made by him; and without him was not any thing made that was made.

—John 1:3

It's easy to praise you for your majesty and power when we see thundering waterfalls, crashing ocean waves, or majestic sunsets. Help us learn to praise you when we see a dewdrop, a seedling, or an ant.

Let the heaven and earth praise him, the seas, and every thing that moveth therein.

—Psalm 69:34

Today I thank you for the beautiful, often mysterious creatures of the seas and oceans. From the intricate ecosystems of tide pools to the massive forms of blue whales, you created it all! I wonder if the joy of dolphins as they flip and spin and play is their way of singing praise to you? I praise you for the marvels of our world!

What shall I render unto the Lord for all his benefits toward me?

—Psalm 116:12

Count your blessings and see how they multiply! Every challenge teaches us something we need to know, which is a blessing. Every obstacle gives us more strength, which is a blessing. Every problem gives us a chance to stretch our minds and come up with a new solution, which is a blessing. All of the good, and all of the lessons of the bad, adds up to an abundance of things to be grateful for.

These things I have spoken unto you, that in me ye might have peace. In the world ye shall have tribulation: but be of good cheer; I have overcome the world.

—John 16:33

God, thank you for sometimes reminding me that in the center of chaos lies the seed of new opportunity and that things are not always as awful as they seem at first. I often forget that what starts out bad can end up great and that it is all a matter of my own perspective. Amen.

July 18

Ointment and perfume rejoice the heart: so doth the sweetness of a man's friend by hearty counsel.

—Proverbs 27:9

What a gift friendship is! I am grateful for my friends. Some friends have known me for many years. We grew up together and watched each other change and grow. Other friends are newer, but no less dear. Thank you, Lord, for all the friends you have placed in my life and for the memories we have created together.

But the fruit of the Spirit is love, joy, peace, longsuffering, gentleness, goodness, faith, Meekness, temperance: against such there is no law.

—Galatians 5:22-23

A kind act by a stranger is a wonderful surprise! I don't expect someone to let me go ahead in line at the store or to return an item I had lost. What a blessing it is when people reach out to others. Thank you for the small acts that make my day better, and thank you for the opportunity to be a blessing to others by finding small ways to make their day brighter.

> Thanks be unto God for his unspeakable gift.
>
> —2 Corinthians 9:15

After making plans to go hiking with friends, I remembered my boots were a half size too small. My budget, however, was telling me that new footwear was out of the question. Without much hope, I decided to visit a sporting-goods store. As I drove there, I spotted a thrift store and felt a strong impulse to stop in. "God, please let there be a good pair of hiking boots in my size here," I prayed. Scanning the rows of shoes, I found only one pair of authentic hiking boots, and they were in new condition. But would they fit? I fumbled to find the sizing information. When I read it, I wanted to let out a whoop, but instead I whispered, "Thank you, God!" Then, handing the cashier a mere eight dollars and some change, I couldn't help but say "Thank you" again.

But godliness with contentment is great gain. For we brought nothing into this world, and it is certain we can carry nothing out. And having food and raiment let us be therewith content.

—1 Timothy 6:6–8

Content with just food and clothing? Really, Lord? I'm thankful that you provide for my basic needs, but there's much, much more on my wish list. This passage makes me realize how much I expect in life. Sometimes I act like I'm entitled to certain things: a well-paying job for little effort on my part, minimal traffic on the way to said job, restaurant lunches every day, seamless relationships with loved ones. Help me to be thankful for the countless blessings in my life and to always be ready to help others rather than focusing on adding to my own stores.

Please guide me, Lord. I'm ready to answer your call to contentment.

How much better is it to get wisdom than gold! and to get understanding rather to be chosen than silver!

—Proverbs 16:16

Lord God, why is it that we tend to hold so tightly to the things of this world? We know in our hearts that everything we have is ours only by your grace and great generosity. When we accumulate more than we need, it only builds barriers between ourselves and you. Thank you for your provision, Lord. May we learn to hold everything loosely, knowing it is only borrowed.

And above all things have fervent charity among yourselves: for charity shall cover the multitude of sins. Use hospitality one to another without grudging.

—1 Peter 4:8-9

In times of trial, I thank you for my friends. Some listen. Some offer distraction by proposing a fun outing. Some bring by food. Some sit quietly with me. I thank you for all the ways they help, big and small. Please let me be such a friend to them!

I have seen his ways, and will heal him: I will lead him also, and restore comforts unto him and to his mourners. I create the fruit of the lips; Peace, peace to him that is far off, and to him that is near, saith the Lord; and I will heal him.

—Isaiah 57:18-19

Lord, thank you for bringing others into our lives to help us heal. We appreciate how much they aid us. Please remind us to thank them for reaching out to us. Thank you for extending your love to us through them. Amen.

Wondrous God, I praise your name.

Your Word is life.

I believe you can heal me.

Be with me when I am sick, and remind me to praise you when I am well.

Thank you for healing me in the past,

And for future healing.

Keep me in good health

That I might serve you

And praise your name.

Amen.

But let it be the hidden man of the heart, in that which is not corruptible, even the ornament of a meek and quiet spirit, which is in the sight of God of great price.

—1 Peter 3:4

Little changes become apparent from year to year in this life. Maybe there's an extra pound or two on our frame. Maybe we've spotted a new gray hair (or two or twenty). Perhaps we suddenly realize we're taking things a little more slowly. As women who belong to God, though, we know these changes are trivial in light of eternity. As our bodies begin to show signs of age, our inner self is growing in radiance, compounding in beauty, flourishing in faith. We are just beginning to blossom within, just beginning to display a bit of the brightness that will burst forth in heaven when our life is finally fully opened to the light of God's love.

Ye also, as lively stones, are built up a spiritual house, an holy priesthood, to offer up spiritual sacrifices, acceptable to God by Jesus Christ.

—1 Peter 2:5

When I read this passage, I think of beautiful polished gemstones and colorful mosaics. You can build us into something truly beautiful! God, it is your love that flows through us, so that we are able to love you and our neighbors. Thank you for making us beautiful to your eyes.

Nevertheless he left not himself without witness, in that he did good, and gave us rain from heaven, and fruitful seasons, filling our hearts with food and gladness.

—Acts 14:17

Rain patters down, making puddles everywhere. I wasn't expecting the rain, but I am grateful for its beauty. I look up and see the thickness of the gray clouds and think of a soft blanket. I listen to the rain pour down and think of how it waters the earth to bring new life. Thank you, Lord, for the gift of a rainy day.

And what is the exceeding greatness of his power to us-ward who believe, according to the working of his mighty power, Which he wrought in Christ, when he raised him from the dead, and set him at his own right hand in the heavenly places.

—Ephesians 1:19-20

Thank you, Lord, for the signs of your power. Thank you for the awe I feel during a thunderstorm or at the sight of a monument in nature. Thank you for the thrill I feel when I see one of your works in all its glory. It is good to know your power and feel its presence in my life.

And God said, Let there be lights in the firmament of the heaven to divide the day from the night; and let them be for signs, and for seasons, and for days, and years.

—Genesis 1:14

Thank you for astronomical wonders. Solar and lunar eclipses, harvest moons, times when a planet is very clearly visible, meteor showers—they all provoke wonder in your creation. Staring up at the sky, I am aware of how small I am, and how grand your works. And even when I am alone, I know others are looking up at the same sky and experiencing that same awe.

The Lord is my strength and song, and he is become my salvation: he is my God, and I will prepare him an habitation; my father's God, and I will exalt him.

—Exodus 15:2

Lord, in my darkest moments, it is easy to despair and fear that you have given up on me. It would be understandable for you to be angry and disappointed and leave me to my ruin. How comforting it is to know that the minute I regret what I have done and turn to you, you are right where you have been all along—by my side, ready to embrace and carry me until I am strong enough to take a step on my own. Thank you for your faithfulness, Lord—especially when I least deserve it.

August

For I am persuaded, that neither death, nor life, nor angels, nor principalities, nor powers, nor things present, nor things to come, Nor height, nor depth, nor any other creature, shall be able to separate us from the love of God, which is in Christ Jesus our Lord.

—Romans 8:38-39

Love indeed makes the world go around and nothing compares to your love. My prayers today are not just for myself, but for all living things, that we may all feel a little more loved, a little more cherished. So many of us go through life thinking we don't matter. I pray your love awakens them to truly understand, as I do, that every single one of us is precious in your sight. I pray love wins over hate and lightens every dark corner. Love is the greatest miracle, Lord, and I am grateful to experience your love daily. Amen.

Now the God of hope fill you with all joy and peace in believing, that ye may abound in hope, through the power of the Holy Ghost.

—Romans 15:13

You, O Lord, are our refuge. When the days are too full and sleep is hard to come by, we simply need to escape to a quiet place and call on you. In your presence we find strength for our work and peace for our troubled minds. We are grateful for the comfort of your embrace, Lord.

But seek ye first the kingdom of God, and his righteousness; and all these things shall be added unto you.

—Matthew 6:33

There is no denying the pleasure of creature comforts. Last year, my husband and I decided to take the plunge and have central air conditioning installed in our old home. Every hot day this summer, I have reveled in returning to a blast of cool air when I get home; on some level, the air conditioning has made my life better. But as much as I appreciate it, I must remember not to be distracted by or consumed by physical comforts to the extent that I neglect my spiritual welfare. Dear God, thank you for air conditioning—it is good to feel good! But may I always be cognizant of well-being on the inside as well as the outside; may my focus on the everlasting rewards of your kingdom be unswerving.

And I have filled him with the spirit of God, in wisdom, and in understanding, and in knowledge, and in all manner of workmanship, To devise cunning works, to work in gold, and in silver, and in brass, And in cutting of stones, to set them, and in carving of timber, to work in all manner of workmanship.

—Exodus 31:3-5

How excited I am when I get a new phone or a new computer! It may be frustrating to learn new techniques, but I am grateful for how they improve my life. Technology helps me stay in touch with people who are far away and share news in an instant. I am grateful for the way technology has made the world a smaller place and how it helps keep people together.

Then shalt thou walk in thy way safely, and thy foot shall not stumble. When thou liest down, thou shalt not be afraid: yea, thou shalt lie down, and thy sleep shall be sweet.

—Proverbs 3:23-24

Too often we hop in our cars or take the bus or train without thinking about how much these ways of transportation make our lives easier. I am grateful for transportation that helps me reach my destinations more quickly. How wonderful it is to get somewhere in just a few minutes or be able to visit someone who lives far away! With every bump of the wheels, may I be grateful for the machines that take me where I need to go.

Like canoeists on the river rapids, O God, we've learned that there is an easy way and a hard way to get through life. Our days are as tumultuous as any rock-strewn river, and life is as frightening as an unstable canoe:

Work—too much or too little. Age—too old or too young. Family—too near or too far. Too little time and money but too much demand. Meanness and violence making us hostages to fear. Stress, tragedy. Shifting values. A rock-strewn life.

It takes a guide and cheering family to make it through both life and river rapids. The hard way, as you remind us, is alone. Cut off from you, cut off from others, we miss the abundant life you promise. Yet running life's course as your child is as life-changing as shooting river rapids. Both require moving into uncertain waters, taking a chance on a guide we can't see, and listening for the encouragement of those we can.

Come, God of wanderers and pilgrims, be our companion and guide. Let prayer be a bridge, a meeting place spanning icy floodwaters. We sense you near and are grateful to no longer be alone, knowing that choosing to live relying on you as our guide is a move as major as paddling onto the deepest, wildest river.

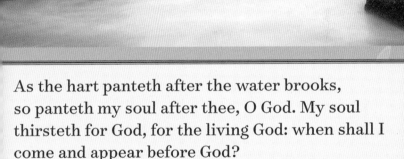

As the hart panteth after the water brooks, so panteth my soul after thee, O God. My soul thirsteth for God, for the living God: when shall I come and appear before God?

—Psalm 42:1–2

We need water to live, but we often don't think about it until times of scarcity—when we have to monitor its use on a camping trip, or find ourselves under a boil order. Let me not take water—or you, the Living Water—for granted, but offer daily gratitude.

And there shall be a tabernacle for a shadow in the day time from the heat, and for a place of refuge, and for a covert from storm and from rain.

—Isaiah 4:6

Bless this roof over our heads, and keep it from leaking. But more than that, move us to give thanks for the next rainstorm. Because you are more than a good roof—we need to remember that. And our neighbors' crops need watering more than we need to stay dry.

And he shall be as the light of the morning, when the sun riseth, even a morning without clouds; as the tender grass springing out of the earth by clear shining after rain.

—2 Samuel 23:4

With boldness and wonder and expectation, I greet you this morning, God of sunrise and rising dew. Gratefully, I look back to all that was good yesterday and in hope, face forward, ready for today.

For by grace are ye saved through faith; and that not of yourselves: it is the gift of God: Not of works, lest any man should boast.

—Ephesians 2:8-9

Lord, how grateful I am that you are willing to go before me to prepare the way. Even when I sense that a new opportunity is from you and has your blessing, I've learned I still need to stop and ask you to lead before I take the first step. Otherwise I will stumble along in the dark tripping over stones of my own creation! Everything goes more smoothly when you are involved, Lord.

Now there are diversities of gifts, but the same Spirit.

—1 Corinthians 12:4

Inspired by you, Great God, and grateful for the unique gifts we're discovering, we toss ourselves into the stream of life to make ripples wherever we are. In your hands, our gifts can offer a gift that keeps on making ever-widening circles to reach all those stranded on shore.

Jesus began to preach, and to say, Repent: for the kingdom of heaven is at hand.

—Matthew 4:17

Lord, I never want to think about my failures. But I know I need to acknowledge my sins—not to wallow in guilt, but to repent and then let go of them. Thank you for holding out your arms in forgiveness. It is a gift that you know my shortcomings and love me anyway. You want me to repent so that you can welcome me into the kingdom!

Nay but, O man, who art thou that repliest against God? Shall the thing formed say to him that formed it, Why hast thou made me thus?

—Romans 9:20

When things go wrong, God is usually the first we blame. Forgive us for even considering that you would deliberately hurt one of your very own children. For what could you possibly have to gain? Thank you for your presence; forgive our easy blame of you.

Let all bitterness, and wrath, and anger, and clamour, and evil speaking, be put away from you, with all malice.

—Ephesians 4:31

Some time ago, a friend drifted away. She became busy with new commitments and had less and less time for our friendship. After a while, I stopped trying to maintain the friendship by myself. When I look back and feel resentful or rejected, please help me to feel grateful instead. While it wasn't a lifelong friendship, it was a good one while it lasted. I ask you to bless her today, and all her endeavors.

Draw nigh to God, and he will draw nigh to you. Cleanse your hands, ye sinners; and purify your hearts, ye double minded.

—James 4:8

Why art thou thus cast down, my heart?

Why troubled, why dost mourn apart,

O'er nought but earthly wealth?

Trust in thy God, be not afraid,

He is thy Friend who all things made.

—Hans Sachs, trans. Catherine Winkworth

O God, thou art life, wisdom, truth, bounty, and blessedness, the eternal, the only true good! My God and my Lord, thou art my hope and my heart's joy. I confess, with thanksgiving, that thou hast made me in thine image, that I may direct all my thoughts to thee, and love thee. Lord, make me to know thee aright, that I may more and more love, and enjoy, and possess thee. And since, in the life here below, I cannot fully attain this blessedness, let it at least grow in me day by day, until it all be fulfilled at last in the life to come. Here be the knowledge of thee increased, and there let it be perfected. Here let my love to thee grow, and there let it ripen; that my joy being here great in hope, may there in fruition be made perfect. Amen.

—St. Anselm

I will praise thee, O Lord, with my whole heart; I will shew forth all thy marvellous works.

—Psalm 9:1

Gratitude may be the most highly underestimated virtue. We think of love, hope, faith, and the power of prayer and forgiveness. But how often do we stop each day and give thanks for all the blessings in our lives? Are we too focused on what we lack, what we don't have, don't want, don't need? By opening the heart and mind to focus on gratitude, we unleash a treasure of unceasing good that's just waiting to overflow into our lives. A grateful person knows that by giving thanks, they're given even more to be thankful for.

A man hath no better thing under the sun, than to eat, and to drink, and to be merry: for that shall abide with him of his labour the days of his life, which God giveth him under the sun.

—Ecclesiastes 8:15

What a joyful noise is the sound of children playing! Thank you for the chance to play with my children, to be silly with them, and to enter their world and share their zest for life. Thank you for allowing me to be young again as I share their joy and their imagination. Thank you for the gift of having a child's joy.

Judge not according to the appearance, but judge righteous judgment.

—John 7:24

I am grateful, O God, that your standards run more to how we're loving you and one another than how we appear. If you judged on lawns, I would be out in the cold! Mine is the yard where kids gather. Ball games, sprinkler tag's muddy marathons, snow fort and tree house constructions, car tinkerings and bike repair—they all happen here. Bless my rutted, littered lawn, wise Creator. It's the most beautiful landscape, dotted as it is with children who will be grown and gone faster than we can say "replant."

August 20

Honour thy father and thy mother, as the Lord thy God hath commanded thee; that thy days may be prolonged, and that it may go well with thee, in the land which the Lord thy God giveth thee.

—Deuteronomy 5:16

Today I am thankful for my family. My parents, my siblings, my cousins and aunts and uncles... all are part of my family and my life. I may not be close to everyone or see everyone as often as I'd like, but I am grateful for their presence in my life. My family is a big part of who I am today. I need to thank them for that gift, even as I thank God for putting these special people in my life.

Thou sittest and speakest against thy brother; thou slanderest thine own mother's son.

—Psalm 50:20

God, I do not intend to hurt you and others. I am not always sure what happens in those times when I do hurt you and others. I am thankful that you forgive. Please help others to forgive me, too. Remind us all to follow your teachings. We pray that you will guide and comfort us.

August 22

> Wherefore, my beloved brethren, let every man be swift to hear, slow to speak, slow to wrath: For the wrath of man worketh not the righteousness of God.
>
> —James 1:19-20

What, God of peace, are we to do with our anger? In the wake of trouble, it fills us to overflowing. Sometimes our anger is the only prayer we can bring you. We are relieved and grateful to know that you are sturdy enough to bear all we feel and say. Where do we go from here? Is there life after fury? What will we be without our anger when it's all that has fueled us? When we are still, we hear your answer: "Emptied." But then we would be nothing. Remind us that, in your redeeming hands, nothing can become of great use, as a gourd hollowed out becomes a cup or a bowl only when emptied. When the time comes for us to empty ourselves of this abundance of anger, make us into something useful. It would be a double tragedy to waste anger's re-creative energy.

A time to weep, and a time to laugh; a time to mourn, and a time to dance.

—Ecclesiastes 3:4

Thank you, Lord, for reddened eyes. Believing your promise that comfort follows mourning, we bawl and sob. In your wisdom, onion-peeling salty tears differ from cleansing grieving ones; we're grateful for their healing. Deliver us from stiff upper lips, and if we've lost our tears, help us find them.

In my distress I called upon the Lord, and cried unto my God: he heard my voice out of his temple, and my cry came before him, even into his ears.

—Psalm 18:6

My guard is constant and vigilant, protecting me against the next episode of my humanness. I know to err is human, but why so often? Peace only comes, God of wholeness, through reassurance that with you, mistakes, errors—even disasters— can yield treasures. I am so grateful.

Rejoice evermore. Pray without ceasing. In every thing give thanks: for this is the will of God in Christ Jesus concerning you.

—1 Thessalonians 5:16-18

Forgive me for complaining, dear God. Help me to remember that every time I have a headache, someone I know may have a hidden heartache; every time I don't like the food, millions have nothing to eat; every time I think my paycheck is small, too many people have no paycheck at all; every time I wish my loved ones were not so demanding, some people have no one to love. When I look around at my blessings, my complaints seem little. Teach me perspective, God, and to be grateful for my everyday gifts of family, food, and home. Amen.

Every moving thing that liveth shall be meat for you; even as the green herb have I given you all things.

—Genesis 9:3

When I go to the supermarket, I am amazed at all the food I find there! As I walk down the store aisles, gratitude fills me for everyone who makes food available to me. I give thanks to the farmers and manufacturers, to those who grow the food and those who package and transport it to me. May I always appreciate their hard work and the bounty they produce.

I am the true vine, and my Father is the husbandman. Every branch in me that beareth not fruit he taketh away: and every branch that beareth fruit, he purgeth it, that it may bring forth more fruit.

—John 15:1-2

Lord, please help me to remember that you are the source of all good things that come out of my life as I grow and flourish in you. All the "good fruit" of love, joy, peace, patience, kindness, goodness, faithfulness, gentleness, and self-control come directly from you and then produce good things in me. I want to thank you for nourishing and supporting my life. Please use the fruit you're producing in me to nourish others and lead them to you as well.

He hath shewed thee, O man, what is good; and what doth the Lord require of thee, but to do justly, and to love mercy, and to walk humbly with thy God?

—Micah 6:8

Lord, if my hunger and thirst for your righteousness could be satisfied by ordering from a spiritual drive-thru, I'd want to supersize my order! I so want to be like Christ. I want to have his courage and humility, his strength and gentleness. I don't want substitutes—such as pride that looks like courage or fear that looks like humility. I want the real deal. Thank you for the promise that you will satisfy this craving of mine, this deep soul hunger to be and do all that is right, true, and good.

Worthy is the Lamb that was slain to receive power, and riches, and wisdom, and strength, and honour, and glory, and blessing.

—Revelation 5:12

When I read this verse, I realize how perfectly Jesus personified heavenly wisdom. It's a wonder to me that we are called to walk in his footsteps, but then I remember that it is only possible to do it through the Spirit that works in and through us. Thank you, Lord, for making the things of heaven available to those who seek them.

Take heed therefore unto yourselves, and to all the flock, over the which the Holy Ghost hath made you overseers, to feed the church of God, which he hath purchased with his own blood.

—Acts 20:28

Father God, when I'm tempted to give up on a task or a ministry opportunity, it helps to read about Abraham, Moses, Joseph, David, Job—all those whose times of trial and perseverance are so beautifully preserved for us through your Word. Once we become attuned to your plan for our lives, we can continue on with the certainty that you always complete what you start. We can stand firmly on your promises, confident that you will give us the strength we need to keep going. Thank you for the faith of the ages, Lord! It is also the faith for today.

Commit thy works unto the Lord, and thy thoughts shall be established.

—Proverbs 16:3

You invented work, God, and I am grateful. Framer of the Cosmos, you've given me a project, too. Creator of the Earth and Oceans, sustain my hands to do it right. Designer of Amoebas and Atoms, give me pause to look after the details. Worker of Ultimate Skill, accomplish your masterwork in my soul this day!

September

The grass withereth, the flower fadeth: but the word of our God shall stand for ever.

—Isaiah 40:8

It's the time of year when we like stews and soups and chili, meals prepared in the slow cooker, where our house smells warm and cozy. Thank you, Lord, for the blessings of this time of year, for warm drinks on crisp days, for the memories of picking apples, for all the joy we see around us.

Keep me as the apple of the eye, hide me under the shadow of thy wings.

—Psalm 17:8

I remember when I was a young child, and the grandmotherly neighbor lit up with delight every time she saw me. How could I resist that joy? Lord, your delight in me is a gift, one that I don't deserve, but one that makes me want to spend time in your presence. Thank you for treating me as a treasure.

Let the word of Christ dwell in you richly in all wisdom; teaching and admonishing one another in psalms and hymns and spiritual songs, singing with grace in your hearts to the Lord.

—Colossians 3:16

Thank you, Lord, for teachers. How can I ever repay the men and women who taught me and opened my eyes to the world? How can I ever truly thank the people who teach my children and guide them on their journey through life? I am so grateful for those who teach and mentor. Thank you for giving us knowledge and wisdom to carry on life's path.

September 4

But the Comforter, which is the Holy Ghost, whom the Father will send in my name, he shall teach you all things, and bring all things to your remembrance, whatsoever I have said unto you.

—John 14:26

Holy Spirit, thank you for all that you have taught me. I am grateful for those times when I have been able to sense your presence, when you have led me to discern the Father's will. And I am grateful for those times when you seemed absent, but looking back, I can see you at work. Please help me trust in your wisdom always.

I thank thee, and praise thee, O thou God of my fathers, who hast given me wisdom and might, and hast made known unto me now what we desired of thee: for thou hast now made known unto us the king's matter.

—Daniel 2:23

Thank you for people who share their wisdom. Sometimes I may think I know everything, but it is good to realize that there are many people who are smarter than me. What a gift to receive their guidance in my life! Help me to have a listening ear and always be grateful for those who want to help me.

Jesus answered and said unto them, Ye do err, not knowing the scriptures, nor the power of God.

—Matthew 22:29

Your son, Jesus, was a reader, Lord. He read from your own books, the Holy Scriptures. Books can change us. They can transport us to other places and other times and can share the wisdom of the ages. I love books and reading and want my children to treasure them, too. Thank you, Lord, for good books, especially the Bible, that can feed our children's minds and imaginations and can show us the wonder of life in your world.

From a child thou hast known the holy scriptures, which are able to make thee wise unto salvation through faith which is in Christ Jesus.

—2 Timothy 3:15

My mother had bookmarks and plaques with favorite Bible verses inscribed on them, and she read from the Bible each and every day. I find it difficult to find the time to do the same, but as I age I'm coming to see it as necessary. When I pray with the scriptures each day, not just in times of crisis or on Sundays, I discover more meaning in them. Those quiet times help my faith deepen and mature. Please instill in me the discipline, Lord, to keep up the habit. Let me always be grateful for the insight your Word offers.

Shew me thy ways, O Lord; teach me thy paths.

—Psalms 25:4

How grateful we are, God of Knowledge, that you created us so curious. In your wisdom, it is the searcher turning over every leaf who finds four-leaf clovers; the doubter who invents; and the determined, like a duckling pecking its way from the shell, who emerges strong enough to fly.

For whatsoever things were written aforetime were written for our learning, that we through patience and comfort of the scriptures might have hope.

—Romans 15:4

I went out recently at a time when the roads were filled with school buses. As I watch children get on the buses that take them to school, I am thankful for my own school days. Thank you, Lord, for my education and the doors it has opened to me. Thank you for the friends I made, the rules I learned, and the teachers who guided me and helped me find my place in the world.

Submit yourselves to every ordinance of man for the Lord's sake: whether it be to the king, as supreme; Or unto governors, as unto them that are sent by him for the punishment of evildoers, and for the praise of them that do well.

—1 Peter 2:13-14

Lord, remind us of a childhood memory of someone in uniform who made a difference in our lives. A school nurse who comforted us, a firefighter who spoke to us on a field trip to the local station, a police officer standing on the neighborhood corner, a doctor who treated us for a childhood illness. Thank you for showing us that someone in uniform could be trusted and could be a friend.

We are troubled on every side, yet not distressed; we are perplexed, but not in despair; Persecuted, but not forsaken; cast down, but not destroyed.

—2 Corinthians 4:8-9

This is a sad and solemn day, yet there is still time to be thankful. Thank you, Lord, for all the emergency workers who help people every day. They bring light to the darkness and help to those who need it most. Thank you for their selflessness and willingness to give everything they have to save another. Just as Jesus sacrificed his life to save us, we are blessed by the sacrifices of those who save our lives.

All things work together for good to them that love God, to them who are the called according to his purpose.

—Romans 8:28

Father, I think about the moments in my life when you changed me. I think about the words that were spoken that gave me a new perspective, a new direction. I think about the angels who stepped into my life and were used by you to show me the way. I think about all these things, and I am grateful. I think about all these words and moments, and I am filled with confidence that you have led me on my way.

So we, being many, are one body in Christ, and every one members one of another.

—Romans 12:5

Thank you, God of inspiration, for the times when you guide me to take my place as an example and a model for my children. For you call us to be loving, tender, and kind. Remind me that this call is more than just creating a family, for the family is Christianity in miniature.

Brethren, I count not myself to have apprehended: but this one thing I do, forgetting those things which are behind, and reaching forth unto those things which are before, I press toward the mark for the prize of the high calling of God in Christ Jesus.

—Philippians 3:13–14

After graduating high school, Anna took a year off to work and earn money for university. "Sometimes it's a little lonely," Anna admits. "Many of my friends have already gone on to college." On low days, Anna feels left behind, but then she reminds herself that this is her path, it's a good one, and that God supports her, always. "God has my back," Anna says simply. "That comforts me."

God, you are my best coach! I don't need to reach higher alone; thank you for being there to inspire me.

This is the confidence that we have in him, that, if we ask any thing according to his will, he heareth us.

—1 John 5:14

We accept your invitation to pray without ceasing. Hear us as we pray boldly, with expectation, believing your assurance that we deserve to be in your presence and to talk all we want. We are grateful that you welcome us at all times and in all places and moods.

To every thing there is a season, and a time to every purpose under the heaven.

—Ecclesiastes 3:1

God, give me peace of mind today, for I am worried about so many things. Give me peace of heart today, for I am fearful of challenges before me. Give me peace of spirit today, for I am in a state of confusion and chaos. I ask, God, for your peace today, and every day, to help keep my feet on the right path and my faith solid and unmoving. Without peace, I don't see the answers you place before me. Without peace, I cannot hear your still, small voice within. Shower me today with your loving peace, God, and all will be well in my mind, heart, and spirit.

Be strong and of a good courage; be not afraid,
neither be thou dismayed: for the Lord thy God is
with thee whithersoever thou goest.

—Joshua 1:9

God's grace is our comfort in times of trouble and
our beacon of hope amid the blackness of despair.
By opening ourselves to God's ever-present grace,
we know we are loved and cared for, and our
hearts sing out in joyful gratitude.

Go your way, eat the fat, and drink the sweet, and send portions unto them for whom nothing is prepared: for this day is holy unto our Lord: neither be ye sorry; for the joy of the Lord is your strength.

—Nehemiah 8:10

Time helps, Lord, but it never quite blunts the loneliness that loss brings. Thank you for the peace that is slowly seeping into my pores, allowing me to live with the unlivable; to bear the unbearable.

Guide and bless my faltering steps down a new road. Prop me up when I think I can't go it alone; prod me when I tarry too long in lonely self-pity.

Most of all, Kind Healer, thank you for the gifts of memory and dreams. The one comforts, the other beckons, both halves of a healing whole.

Beloved, be not ignorant of this one thing, that one day is with the Lord as a thousand years, and a thousand years as one day.

—2 Peter 3:8

Look at the clock. What time is it? Is it time to go? Are we running out of time? I need more time! Lord, help me to stop and relax and enjoy time instead of feeling like it is my enemy. Help me be grateful for each minute and the special joys it brings. Sometimes I need to slow down and think of time as my friend. Thank you, Lord, for time and the gifts it brings me.

Remember ye not the former things, neither consider the things of old. Behold, I will do a new thing; now it shall spring forth; shall ye not know it? I will even make a way in the wilderness, and rivers in the desert.

—Isaiah 43:18-19

Just when I settle in with one reality, something new disrupts. Overnight change, God of all the time in the world, is comforting and grief-making, for it's a reminder that nothing stays the same. Not tough times, not good ones either. Despite today's annoyance, I'm grateful for change, assured it will take me to new moments you have in mind.

They that sow in tears shall reap in joy. He that goeth forth and weepeth, bearing precious seed, shall doubtless come again with rejoicing, bringing his sheaves with him.

—Psalm 126:5-6

Lord, I see you in the beauty of the autumn. Thank you for the brilliant colors of the trees. Thank you for the crisp, cool air that refreshes me. I am blessed to see autumn's beauty everywhere I go. Thank you for showing me that a time of change can be one of the most gorgeous seasons on Earth.

With grateful heart my thanks I bring,

before the great your praise I sing;

I worship in your holy place

and praise you for your truth and grace;

for truth and grace together shine

in your most holy word divine,

in your most holy word divine.

—"With Grateful Heart My Thanks I Bring"

I cried to you, and you did save;

your word of grace new courage gave;

the kings of earth shall thank you, Lord,

for they have heard your wondrous word;

yea, they shall come with songs of praise,

for great and glorious are your ways,

for great and glorious are your ways.

—"With Grateful Heart My Thanks I Bring"

Peace I leave with you, my peace I give unto you: not as the world giveth, give I unto you. Let not your heart be troubled, neither let it be afraid.

—John 14:27

No matter the worries I have, small or large, you, O God, are there ahead of me with promises of help and support that relieve me and free me from getting stuck in the mire of my fear. I am grateful.

They that wait upon the Lord shall renew their strength; they shall mount up with wings as eagles; they shall run, and not be weary; and they shall walk, and not faint.

—Isaiah 40:31

How lonely we are when trouble strikes. Send us a sign, Lord. We long for a message, a hand reaching toward us. And just as God promised, we're visited by a Presence in dream and daylight revelations, and we are grateful for God's personal, one-on-one caring.

Ye shall seek me, and find me, when ye shall search for me with all your heart.

—Jeremiah 29:13

Father, I thank you for the spiritual restlessness that drives me to seek a deeper relationship with you. Sometimes I try to fill what I perceive as gaps in my life with other things—work, hobbies, social media. I shy away from feeling incomplete. Let me fill my life with those gifts that are from you, God, and let me continue to seek you instead of settling for substitutes that seem to nourish or entertain for a while but ultimately do not satisfy.

Take heed, and beware of covetousness: for a man's life consisteth not in the abundance of the things which he possesseth.

—Luke 12:15

Lord, I've stood by too many deathbeds to ever doubt that the adage "you can't take it with you" is absolutely true. We come into this world with nothing, and we leave with nothing. So why is it so tempting to spend so much of our lifetimes striving for more money and possessions? We forget that all those things are fleeting, and that the only people who are impressed by what we accumulate are those whose values are worldly. But you, O God, are eternal! Thank you for providing a way for us to be with you forever.

> The Lord recompense thy work, and a full reward be given thee of the Lord God of Israel, under whose wings thou art come to trust.
>
> —Ruth 2:12

Work is good right now, God of all labor, and I think I know why: You and I are working together. Is this what it is to be called?

I think it must be, for you are the source of my talents, for which I am grateful. Through the support of others, gifted teachers, mentors, and leaders, and through those willing to take a chance on me despite the odds, you have always been present, and I am grateful for that, too.

Although this sense that I am doing what you intend for me is usually just a delicious, split-second awareness, O God, it is enough to keep me going when I am tired, frustrated, and unclear about my next step. Our companionship of call to vocation is not an instant process, but rather a shared journey. Keep me listening, watching.

I am glad we share this working venture, for on the job and off, I am blessed.

We glory in tribulations also: knowing that tribulation worketh patience; And patience, experience; and experience, hope: And hope maketh not ashamed; because the love of God is shed abroad in our hearts by the Holy Ghost which is given unto us.

—Romans 5:3-5

Life's not fair, and I stomp my foot in frustration. The powerful get more so as the rest of us shrink, dreams for peace are shattered as bullies get the upper hand, and despair is as tempting as an ice cream sundae. Help me hold on, for you are a God of justice and dreams, of turning life upside down. Let me help; thanks for listening in the meantime.

September 30

Wherefore we receiving a kingdom which cannot be moved, let us have grace, whereby we may serve God acceptably with reverence and godly fear: For our God is a consuming fire.

—Hebrews 12:28-29

Thank you, Lord, thank you, Lord,
thank you, Lord,
I just want to thank you, Lord.
Been so good, been so good,
been so good,
I just want to thank you, Lord.
—Traditional

October

My shepherd is the living Lord:
now shall my needs be well supplied;
his loving care and holy word
will be my safety and my guide.

In pastures where salvation grows
he makes me feed, he gives me rest;
there living water gently flows,
and food is given, divinely blest.

Though I walk through the gloomy vale
where death and all its terrors are,
my heart and hope shall never fail:
my shepherd holds me in his care.

Amid the darkness and the deeps,
God is my comfort, God my stay;
his staff supports my feeble steps,
his rod directs my doubt-filled way.

Surely the mercies of the Lord
attend his household all their days;
there will I dwell, to hear his word,
to seek his face, to sing his praise.
—Isaac Watts

Know therefore that the Lord thy God, he is God, the faithful God, which keepeth covenant and mercy with them that love him and keep his commandments to a thousand generations.

—Deuteronomy 7:9

God, it's easier to express gratitude for your love when things are going well than when I'm dealing with tough issues. But even when I can't rely on anything else, I can rely on your love. I thank you for how you stand by me even in times of trouble.

I will restore health unto thee, and I will heal thee of thy wounds, saith the Lord; because they called thee an Outcast, saying, This is Zion, whom no man seeketh after.

—Jeremiah 30:17

Lord, this healing process is sometimes slow, and I get discouraged and filled with doubt. Can I take this? Will I make it? Yet you always remind me of your powerful presence and assure me that where I am unable to go, you will go for me and what I am unable to do by myself, you will do for me. Thank you, Lord. Amen.

Bless the Lord, O my soul, and forget not all his benefits: Who forgiveth all thine iniquities; who healeth all thy diseases; Who redeemeth thy life from destruction; who crowneth thee with lovingkindness and tender mercies.

—Psalm 103:2-4

Today I thank you for medical professionals: doctors and nurses and technicians. I ask you to bless them, to give them the gift of being compassionate with their patients, to help them say the right words when breaking bad news. I ask you to protect and shield them from burnout, that they have the support they need in their own lives to heal from the difficult times they go through. Please help them know that you are always with them, Our Great Physician.

O Lord my God, I cried unto thee, and thou hast healed me. O Lord, thou hast brought up my soul from the grave: thou hast kept me alive, that I should not go down to the pit.

—Psalm 30:2-3

Dear God,

I come to you today humbled and grateful for the powerful healing you have given me. I was so ill and broken, and weak in body and spirit, and I was losing my faith that I would ever feel good again. Yet you took care of me. Your love provided me with all the medicine I could ever need, and the hope of your eternal presence motivated me to stay in faith, even when things seemed so bleak. I thank you from the bottom of my heart for this new sense of well-being and health, and for knowing that if I stay positive and hopeful, your loving will for me will prevail over any disease or challenge. Amen.

Be strong and of a good courage, fear not, nor be afraid of them: for the Lord thy God, he it is that doth go with thee; he will not fail thee, nor forsake thee.

—Deuteronomy 31:6

Dear Lord,

I ask in prayer today for courage and strength to face some big challenges before me. I admit I am anxious, and even afraid, but I know in my heart you will never give me anything I cannot handle, and that you will be by my side the whole way. Instill in me a strong heart and spirit as I deal with my problems and keep my mind centered and focused on the solutions you set before me. I ask nothing more than your presence alongside me as I overcome these obstacles and learn the lessons each one has for my life. I thank you, Lord, for always being there for me in my times of need and struggle. Amen.

The trial of your faith, being much more precious than of gold that perisheth, though it be tried with fire, might be found unto praise and honour and glory at the appearing of Jesus Christ.

—1 Peter 1:7

Lord, you know how all-encompassing grief can be. The weight we carry is physical as well as emotional, and even getting up in the morning can seem like an impossible, pointless act. Thank you, Lord, for bringing us comfort during such times. Eventually the day comes when we have the pleasant realization that we actually feel a little invigorated. We hold our heads a little higher as you help us find joy in our memories and peace in the knowledge that our loved one is safe by your side, looking down on us over your shoulder.

They continued stedfastly in the apostles' doctrine and fellowship, and in breaking of bread, and in prayers. And fear came upon every soul: and many wonders and signs were done by the apostles. And all that believed were together, and had all things common.

—Acts 2:42-44

Lord, today my heart is full of gratitude for your church. Thank you for asking us to meet together to honor you. What power there is in voicing our thanks and petitions together! What comfort in the outstretched arms of friends! Protect us, Lord. Keep us strong—now and in the days to come.

The Lord God formed man of the dust of the ground, and breathed into his nostrils the breath of life; and man became a living soul.

—Genesis 2:7

Every moment we are alive is full of reasons to sing out in joyful gratitude. Every breath we are given is a reminder that the glory of life is at hand. In the people we love, in the beauty of nature, in the golden sun that rises each morning—miracles are everywhere.

For nature around me, I thank you.

For grass and tree, I thank you.

For sun and rain, I thank you.

For fields of grain, I thank you.

For cloudy skies, I thank you.

For mountain highs, I thank you.

For desert flowers, I thank you.

For twilight hours, I thank you.

Tom struggled to find time for prayer. The mornings were rushed with getting the kids out the door to school. He needed to pay attention to the road during his commute to and from work, and work itself kept him busy. By the end of the day, after getting the kids to bed, he and his wife were tired and in no mood to pray. The family attended church services on Sunday, but it was hard to see God's presence throughout the week.

But then there was a scare with one of the children—Tom got a phone call that there had been a car accident while his daughter was carpooling home from a sports activity. As Tom rushed to the hospital, he prayed. When his daughter was fine, just shaken up, he thanked God. And in the days after, he made a new effort to pray throughout the day, and asked for God's grace in sustaining that effort.

God, grant us the grace to turn to you, to find opportunities for prayer throughout the day.

Continue in prayer, and watch in the same with thanksgiving.

—Colossians 4:2

Father, I pray today for a clear path, a strong wind at my back pushing me forward, and the courage of a lion to step into greatness. I am afraid and uncomfortable, but with you I can begin the journey of a thousand miles—with one bold step. Thank you for the powerful gift of prayer.

I will endeavour that ye may be able after my decease to have these things always in remembrance.

—2 Peter 1:15

The past does not have to be an enemy, Rather, let it be a friend and an ally that reminds you of where you've been, how far you've come, and what you've learned along the way. Then let it go as you would a favorite but little-used old garment, with love and gratitude, knowing that God will always provide you with something wonderful and new to wear along the way.

Therefore if any man be in Christ, he is a new creature: old things are passed away; behold, all things are become new.

—2 Corinthians 5:17

Lord, sometimes I think back to who I was before I knew you, and I don't even recognize myself. That's how great the change is when you make us new creations! I'm so glad that the person I was isn't nearly as important in your eyes as the person you know I can be. I may have been younger and fitter then, but I was lost on this worldly adventure. Thank you, Lord, for claiming me as your own and making everything new in my life!

This I recall to my mind, therefore have I hope. It is of the Lord's mercies that we are not consumed, because his compassions fail not. They are new every morning: great is thy faithfulness.

—Lamentations 3:21-23

How often do we make plans, only to have them fall apart? When my day doesn't turn out the way I planned, it's easy to become angry. Instead, I look for ways to make the day special in a different way and thank God for showing me a new path. Lord, teach me to have a flexible heart and be willing to spend my time as you see fit, not as I do, and to open my eyes to the beauty of the unexpected.

Be thou partaker of the afflictions of the gospel according to the power of God; Who hath saved us, and called us with an holy calling, not according to our works, but according to his own purpose and grace, which was given us in Christ Jesus before the world began.

—2 Timothy 1:8-9

Every day I blow it. Every day I need your grace, Lord. I am thankful that it isn't necessary to live a perfect life to have access to your grace. If that were the case, I'd be in big trouble. But instead of turning your back on me when I veer from your paths, you are always ready to welcome me with open arms. You simply call me to trust in your saving, relationship-restoring grace. That's where I'm standing right now—in that amazing grace of yours, asking you to forgive and restore me once again so I can resume good fellowship with you.

Lord Jesus Christ, in thee alone,

My only hope on earth I place,

For other comforter is none,

No help have I but in thy grace.

There is no man nor creature here,

No angel in the heav'nly sphere,

Who at my call can succor me.

I cry to thee,

In thee I trust implicitly.

—Johannes Schneesing, trans. Catherine
Winkworth

Only fear the Lord, and serve him in truth with all your heart: for consider how great things he hath done for you.

—1 Samuel 12:24

When did you last pause to recognize God's wisdom in the timing of events in your life? Have you thanked him? There's so much to be grateful for in this life! Thank you, God, for your many blessings.

Fear none of those things which thou shalt suffer: behold, the devil shall cast some of you into prison, that ye may be tried; and ye shall have tribulation ten days: be thou faithful unto death, and I will give thee a crown of life.

—Revelation 2:10

Dear Lord,

I pray for a strong spirit to stand against my fears today. I don't ask for fearlessness, because I do feel fear, and I do worry and doubt and I am human. Instead, I pray that you will be at my side in frightening situations, and that you will never leave me abandoned and forgotten. I pray you will shore up my own spirit and give me a sharp mind and deep faith, so that I can overcome any blocks in the road to love, peace and happiness. Lord, stand beside me, and hold my hand, but also give me that extra bit of courage for the times you ask that I walk through the darkness alone. Thank you, Lord. Amen.

He that is slow to wrath is of great understanding: but he that is hasty of spirit exalteth folly.

—Proverbs 14:29

Why am I so contrary? I wonder and worry. Perhaps it is tiredness, frustration, pressure, but too often I lose my cool and then the children do likewise until we have a mess and muddle. I'm so grateful that God can help repair it.

Ye shall know the truth, and the truth shall make you free.

—John 8:32

Life has made the most hopeful among us skeptical, Lord of truth. Much is bogus, and we are uncertain. Thank you for the gift of doubt, for it sparks our seeking. Keep us lively and excited as we set off on quests blessed by you, heeding your advice to knock, seek, ask.

Lying lips are abomination to the Lord: but they that deal truly are his delight.

—Proverbs 12:22

Lord, today a little white lie slipped out of my mouth to save me from a trying commitment. As soon as I felt your little tug on my conscience, I knew I had to come clean about it and repair my relationship with you and with my friend.

I know that the lie wasn't small in your eyes, and it was a reminder to me that I am always vulnerable to sin. If I didn't feel your nudge to repair the situation as quickly as possible, I might have fallen into a complacency that would make me vulnerable to any number of more serious sins. I thank you for nudging me, Lord, and for forgiving me, yet again.

Who is a God like unto thee, that pardoneth iniquity, and passeth by the transgression of the remnant of his heritage? he retaineth not his anger for ever, because he delighteth in mercy.

—Micah 7:18

Lord, only you can take all the heartaches and failures in our lives and turn them into compassionate messages of hope for others. We care for an aging parent who passes away, and so are able to relate to the needs of the elderly around us. We go through a divorce, and we can then give genuine advice during our interactions with single mothers. Our pain becomes others' gain, Lord. Sometimes looking back over our shoulders brings us hope for the opportunities that are surely ahead of us. Thank you for second chances.

Be ye kind one to another, tenderhearted, forgiving one another, even as God for Christ's sake hath forgiven you.

—Ephesians 4:32

Sometimes the smallest gesture can mean so much. I thank you today, Lord, for the smile from a stranger, for the grandchild who wants to share a cookie, for the friend who reached out "just because." I thank you for the colleague who paid a compliment on a new haircut, the spouse who emptied the dishwasher when it was my turn, the teenaged rebel who gave me a hug.

For clean air and pure water; for glorious colors in sky and tree in first and last bloom, in the wings of migrating bird. Lord of all, to you we raise our hymn of grateful praise.

For wildlife sanctuaries, open range, prairies, mountains; for backyard gardens; for corn stalks and bean stems growing tall then bending low for harvest. For your generous gifts that meet human need. Lord of all, to you we raise our hymn of grateful praise.

Every day and night we marvel at your wondrous care. Constantly you guide our choices, inviting us to creative living. All creation reflects your empowering love: rolling countryside, stark canyons, majestic mountains, and delicate wildflowers. Sunrise and star, warmth and chill all declare your glory, singing together. Lord of all, to you we raise our hymn of grateful praise.

For love that gives us soul-satisfying happiness; for families, friends, and all others around us; for loved ones here and loved ones beyond; for tender, peaceful thoughts. Lord of all, to you we raise our hymn of grateful praise.

Not that I speak in respect of want: for I have learned, in whatsoever state I am, therewith to be content. I know both how to be abased, and I know how to abound: every where and in all things I am instructed both to be full and to be hungry, both to abound and to suffer need. I can do all things through Christ which strengtheneth me.

—Philippians 4:11–13

Cherish the chance to work and play and think and speak and sing; all simple pleasures are opportunities for grateful praise.

Even every one that is called by my name: for I have created him for my glory, I have formed him; yea, I have made him.

—Isaiah 43:7

When Angela's son Kevin left for college, Angela was surprised to discover the extent to which she felt at loose ends. "I was still working as a nurse then," she remembers, "but with Kevin successfully out in the world, I felt a lack of motivation." Reexamining her faith helped. "I began by thanking God for Kevin's happiness—the way he was spreading his wings," she says now. "Glorifying God in this way restored to me a feeling of purpose."

God, when I'm feeling down about myself and my purpose in life, may I remember to glorify you—that is my purpose!

Seest thou a man diligent in his business? he shall stand before kings; he shall not stand before mean men.

—Proverbs 22:29

How good to get this promotion! And how I've waited for this day! Now that it is here, I thank you for the chance to savor it. A job well done is a good thing, I know. I will celebrate before your smiling eyes and give you credit, too. Because, after all, everything I am and have comes from your gracious hand.

He hath made every thing beautiful in his time: also he hath set the world in their heart, so that no man can find out the work that God maketh from the beginning to the end.

—Ecclesiastes 3:11

Keep us from being slaves to time, Lord. You always create time and space for anything we are doing that brings you glory. Teach us to rest in the knowledge that time is in your hands. Whenever we think we don't have enough of it, show us you have plenty and are happy to share! Thank you, Lord, for your generous supply of time.

Grow in grace, and in the knowledge of our Lord and Saviour Jesus Christ. To him be glory both now and for ever. Amen.

—2 Peter 3:18

Just yesterday, the children

were babies; overnight,

they have jobs, homes,

and babies of their own.

"Overnight" change, Lord,

is comforting, though, reminding me

that nothing stays the same.

Not tough times, not good ones,

just the blending

of one stage into another.

I am grateful for the movement

with you at my side.

Fear thou not; for I am with thee: be not dismayed; for I am thy God: I will strengthen thee; yea, I will help thee; yea, I will uphold thee with the right hand of my righteousness.

—Isaiah 41:10

Happy Halloween! Even though Halloween is built around fear, it can also be a time of joy and gratitude. Thank you for the joy I feel when I see children dressed in costume and enjoying their special night. Thank you for a day when everyone can be as weird as they want to be. Thank you for letting us celebrate the unusual and see the world in a different way.

November

I will sacrifice unto thee with the voice of thanksgiving; I will pay that that I have vowed. Salvation is of the Lord.

—Jonah 2:9

O Lord, as we enter this season of thanksgiving, how important it is for us to grasp the concept of "enough." You know how this world tempts us with all that is bigger, better—more in every way! But there is such joy and freedom in trusting that you will give us exactly what we need—neither too little nor too much. May we never take for granted all the blessings we have, Lord, and may we be as generous with others as you are with us. It is the simple life that brings us closest to you; we are blessed when we live simply.

Blessed are they that mourn: for they shall be comforted.

—Matthew 5:4

When I drift away from you, it is often sorrow and need that draw me back. In times of crisis, I instinctively turn towards you. Thank you for sending your Spirit of consolation. Let me always remember that gratitude.

When the Lord saw her, he had compassion on her, and said unto her, Weep not. And he came and touched the bier: and they that bare him stood still. And he said, Young man, I say unto thee, Arise.

—Luke 7:13–14

The widow whose only son died didn't even need to ask Jesus for help. When he saw her desperate grief, he reached out to perform a miracle. I can only imagine her incredulous joy, and how startled and amazed all the mourners must have been.

Those who were bearing the bier must have seen something in this stranger who came to them, that they halted when Jesus came close. May I be attuned to your presence, Jesus, that I stop to allow you to work. I thank you, Jesus, for the unexpected gifts you have given me.

God shall wipe away all tears from their eyes; and there shall be no more death, neither sorrow, nor crying, neither shall there be any more pain: for the former things are passed away.

—Revelation 21:4

Lord, only you can comfort us when we grieve. The heaviness we feel at such times can make even breathing a struggle. But you, O Lord, stay close. You fill us with your peace and your comfort. You never let us retreat completely from your light into the darkness of despair. And finally, in your time, you restore joy to our souls. We are ever so grateful, O Great Comforter.

I will remember the works of the Lord: surely I will remember thy wonders of old. I will meditate also of all thy work, and talk of thy doings.

—Psalm 77:11-12

Lord, you have told us to "remember the days of old." We thank you for these reminders to honor the past. As we remember those who have gone before us, we teach our children love and respect for life itself. In giving honor to others, we thank and honor you, O God, for your love and for the great sacrifice of your son, Jesus Christ.

Hear counsel, and receive instruction, that thou mayest be wise in thy latter end.

—Proverbs 19:20

Thank you, God, for the wisdom to know when to speak, what to say, and how to say it. Guard my mouth today from any form of foolishness, that in all circumstances I might honor you with my words.

We are his workmanship, created in Christ Jesus unto good works, which God hath before ordained that we should walk in them.

—Ephesians 2:10

Today I will find a way to share my gifts with others. It might be something small, but I want to find a way to give something of myself. Thank you, Lord, for being able to share our gifts and for being givers. Even a small gift is a blessing, and I am grateful to both give and receive.

The Lord shall open unto thee his good treasure, the heaven to give the rain unto thy land in his season, and to bless all the work of thine hand: and thou shalt lend unto many nations, and thou shalt not borrow.

—Deuteronomy 28:12

Thank you for the gift of writing. What a joy it is to express myself through words! A letter, a diary entry, a blog, or a report... all these things are ways I can share my thoughts and knowledge with the world. I am grateful for the chance to express myself and pray that God will guide my pen every time I write.

Oh that my words were now written! oh that they were printed in a book! That they were graven with an iron pen and lead in the rock for ever!

—Job 19:23-24

What a wonderful gift a book is! Thank you, Lord, for the gift of books, for words and poetry and stories. When I pick up a good book, I am taken away to another place and have the chance to meet amazing people. Thank you for the writers who create the books I love and who have invited me into their worlds.

Trust in the Lord with all thine heart; and lean not unto thine own understanding. In all thy ways acknowledge him, and he shall direct thy paths.

—Proverbs 3:5-6

God, let me thank you for all of the times you've pushed me forward when I wanted to stop. For the days when I thought I could not continue, thank you for giving me the shove I needed to break on through. With you, I can go on and fight the good fight!

Greater love hath no man than this, that a man lay down his life for his friends.

—John 15:13

Thank you for our veterans and those who serve in the military. May I always remember those who have given up their day-to-day lives just to keep me and my country safe and secure. Help me to show my gratitude toward the veterans I meet and always remember to honor their sacrifices.

The Lord is faithful, who shall stablish you, and keep you from evil.

—2 Thessalonians 3:3

God, when life feels like a ride that won't let us off, remind us that you are waiting for us to reach up to you. And when we finally do, thank you for being there to lift us to peace and safety.

Let him that stole steal no more: but rather let him labour, working with his hands the thing which is good, that he may have to give to him that needeth.

—Ephesians 4:28

I thank you for my work, Lord. And please bless me in it. Most of all, help me to remember that the paycheck worth working for consists of more than just money. It must include meaning and significance, for myself and others.

According to the grace of God which is given unto me, as a wise masterbuilder, I have laid the foundation, and another buildeth thereon. But let every man take heed how he buildeth thereupon.

—1 Corinthians 3:10

Sometimes lunchtime on the job feels like a family reunion. Our coworkers feel like family and we are grateful to belong. What a blessing to be members of a creative, caring unit—caring about the business and those who make it happen. Productivity is up as lifted morale provides the momentum to do more and do it better, byproducts we take home. Bless the folks down the hall, across the room, in the next department, or in the office next door. They are more than coworkers, they are workaday neighbors.

Her children arise up, and call her blessed; her husband also, and he praiseth her.

—Proverbs 31:28

This morning there were, as my grandfather used to say, a lot of moving parts. My husband needed to catch an early train into the city, my son Ben couldn't find his chemistry textbook, and our dog scarfed down the bread I'd intended for everyone's lunch sandwiches. I was feeling pretty frazzled, and had to get to work myself. But after the boys got out the door and I'd made sure the dog was none the worse for wear, I took a deep breath and noticed that Ben had made me a pot of coffee before leaving for school. My husband had promised he'd order us a pizza tonight so that no one had to cook. And our dog? Well, it's hard to stay mad at a smiling dog!

Lord, even when things are a little crazy around our house, I thank you: I am blessed by my family.

The Lord thy God in the midst of thee is mighty; he will save, he will rejoice over thee with joy; he will rest in his love, he will joy over thee with singing.

—Zephaniah 3:17

Love. It seems so simple. Love is a gift given. Yet, if we don't overlook it, Lord, we treat it like a gift certificate saved so long it expires. We are down-on-our-knees grateful your gifts of love and grace never expire. Nudge us to use them, for we lose their value each day they go unclaimed. We stay disconnected from you, the source of creation and re-creation. To connect only requires a "Yes!" from us. Hear us shout!

> But Moses hands were heavy; and they took a stone, and put it under him, and he sat thereon; and Aaron and Hur stayed up his hands, the one on the one side, and the other on the other side; and his hands were steady until the going down of the sun.
>
> —Exodus 17:12

Though Tracy's mom has limited mobility, she's still game for adventure. And Tracy, at 60, is grateful she still has the strength to take her mom out. "It can be a big production," Tracy says. "It'll be snowing, and getting my mom in and out of the car with the chair can be tiring. But I'm glad I can still do it: we go out for coffee at our favorite diner, or we'll go shopping together. It's always worth it!"

God, sometimes uplifting others means offering actual physical help. Please grant me the literal strength to be able to do so!

There was a man in Jerusalem, whose name was Simeon; and the same man was just and devout, waiting for the consolation of Israel: and the Holy Ghost was upon him.

—Luke 2:25

Thank you for our elders, those grandparents and great-aunts and uncles who have modeled faith and generosity to us! Thank you for those stalwart members of our faith community who, like Anna and Simeon, have grown deep in their faith over their long lives, acting as a beacon to us.

He causeth the grass to grow for the cattle, and herb for the service of man: that he may bring forth food out of the earth.

—Psalm 104:14

The bread is baking in the oven, and our home smells wonderful. Thank you for the pleasure we take in the process of baking, the anticipation as we wait for the result, and the nourishment this food will offer.

He that ministereth seed to the sower both minister bread for your food, and multiply your seed sown, and increase the fruits of your righteousness.

—2 Corinthians 9:10

Thank you, Lord, at the harvest time. Thank you for the plants that grow to give us food and thank you for the people who grow them. The Earth's bounty is a miracle! As I enjoy fresh food, may I always be grateful for what I eat and the nutrition it provides.

Praise the Lord, call upon his name, declare his doings among the people, make mention that his name is exalted. Sing unto the Lord; for he hath done excellent things: this is known in all the earth.

—Isaiah 12:4-5

Thanksgiving is almost here, and Advent and Christmas will follow! Lord, during this season let me stay focused on you. Let me be truly thankful for my blessings, and not so intent on throwing the perfect party or preparing the best meal that I forget to be kind to my family and friends. Thank you for the gifts of faith, family, and friends!

And Elijah said unto Elisha, Tarry here, I pray thee; for the Lord hath sent me to Bethel. And Elisha said unto him, As the Lord liveth, and as thy soul liveth, I will not leave thee. So they went down to Bethel.

—2 Kings 2:2

God gives us strength to go with our friends and share their burdens and responsibilities. When my friend and mentor, Diane, needed to travel to a cancer clinic in another city, I felt called to accompany her. I could not change her diagnosis, but I could be there, as a friend and companion, as she has been there for me these many years.

Dear God, thank you for the powerful gift of friendship. May I tap into your strength to be steadfast and true to my friends; as Elisha accompanied Elijah, may I walk beside my friends in good times and bad.

November 23

Come unto me, all ye that labour and are heavy laden, and I will give you rest.

—Matthew 11:28

As the days grow colder and darker, I ask your blessing on those who suffer from the cold: the homeless, those whose furnace went out at the worst time, those who are struggling to pay the heating bill. Please keep them safe, and please motivate the rest of us to help in some way. Lord, thank you for being a God of comfort and caring.

Now in a song of grateful praise,

To thee, O Lord, my voice I'll raise:

With all thy Saints I'll join to tell,

My Jesus has done all things well.

And above the rest this note shall swell,

This note shall swell, this note shall swell,

And above the rest this note shall swell,

My Jesus has done all things well.

—Samuel Medley

Oh that men would praise the Lord for his goodness, and for his wonderful works to the children of men! For he satisfieth the longing soul, and filleth the hungry soul with goodness.

—Psalm 107:8-9

Lord, each day you furnish us with our daily bread. You feed and nourish us, yet often we neglect to acknowledge your gifts of food.

Forgive us, Father, for our selfishness and our disregard for your faithful care. We know that prayer should be a necessary part of every meal.

If, in our haste, we forget to thank you, Lord, remind us of our rudeness. Our meals are not complete until we thank the giver for his many gifts.

Give us this day our daily bread.

—Matthew 6:11

Thank you for sustaining food, from plain oatmeal for everyday breakfasts to exquisite chocolates for special occasions. Thank you for shared meals with family and friends, where we also share what's going on in our lives. Whatever we eat, ultimately it is your love for us that sustains us.

The light of the eyes rejoiceth the heart: and a good report maketh the bones fat.

—Proverbs 15:30

In the evening and morning and noonday we praise thee, we thank thee, and pray thee, Master of all, to direct our prayers as incense before thee. Let not our hearts turn away to words or thoughts of wickedness, but keep us from all things that might hurt us; for to thee, O Lord, our eyes look up, and our hope is in thee: confound us not, O our God; for the sake of Jesus Christ our Lord.

—Third Century Christian Prayer

Whatsoever ye do in word or deed, do all in the name of the Lord Jesus, giving thanks to God and the Father by him.

—Colossians 3:17

Let's revive the custom of blessing. When we bless someone, we show love and respect, encourage greatness and pride. Sincerely honoring the people and things in our lives is a wonderful way of showing gratitude to the Lord.

Behold, how good and how pleasant it is for brethren to dwell together in unity!

—Psalm 133:1

Dear God, shine through me and help me lighten another's darkness by showing the same friendship that you extended. Show me a person that is in desperate need of a friend today. Help me to be sensitive, caring, and willing to go out of my way to meet this person's need right now, whether it be emotional, physical, or spiritual. Thank you that when I need a friend, YOU are the friend that sticketh closer than a brother. In Jesus' name, Amen.

The Lord shall guide thee continually, and satisfy thy soul in drought, and make fat thy bones: and thou shalt be like a watered garden, and like a spring of water, whose waters fail not.

—Isaiah 58:11

Today, in the dreary days as we head toward winter, I celebrate flowers. How wonderful it is to see their bright colors. I am grateful for the chance to bring flowers into my home to brighten a dreary day. Thank you for the colors and smells of spring and the opportunity to welcome them into my life at any time of year.

December

To do good and to communicate forget not: for with such sacrifices God is well pleased.

—Hebrews 13:16

Lord, sometimes I feel guilty that I haven't thanked you enough for the blessings in my life. I know I possess luxuries that others merely wish for. In this cold month of December I am grateful for the roof over my head, the heated seats in my car, and the warmth of my family and friends. Remind me not to take these kindnesses for granted and help when I see someone in need.

December 2

We are bound to thank God always for you, brethren, as it is meet, because that your faith groweth exceedingly, and the charity of every one of you all toward each other aboundeth.

—2 Thessalonians 1:3

Bless us in this time of good fortune. Give us the grace to be grateful for newfound comforts, magnanimous among those who have less, and thoroughly giving with all we've been given. Amen.

We love him, because he first loved us.

—1 John 4:19

Lord, thank you for heirlooms. The rocking chair where I remember sitting on Grandma's lap, and then rocking my own child, is now being passed down. I cherish the thought of every moment I will hold my own grandchild. I thank you for all these connections to the past and these legacies of love, for all love flows ultimately from you.

December 4

Therefore, brethren, stand fast, and hold the traditions which ye have been taught, whether by word, or our epistle.

—2 Thessalonians 2:15

Taking part in family traditions is such a joyous experience! Today I will take time to recall the traditions I experienced as a child and the family times I shared with those around me. I am grateful for those memories and for the opportunity to share those traditions with my family and friends today. Continuing a tradition feels like taking joyful steps along a path from the past to the future.

Blessed are the pure in heart: for they shall see God.

—Matthew 5:8

When I read this beatitude, I think of my grandmother and her warm, radiant smile. Though she was a busy woman with a number of hobbies, she spent time in prayer every morning and every evening, and that prayer time was her spiritual anchor. More than that, when she saw something beautiful, she spontaneously praised God. When something good happened, words of gratitude sprang from her lips. What a beautiful example she was, of someone in tune with God's will.

Children's children are the crown of old men; and the glory of children are their fathers.

—Proverbs 17:6

Once again, a little child is leading. I had become so serious; all I knew were tasks behind, tasks ahead—until the grandbaby threw me a ball to chase. There I went, like some silly old fool. But chase it I did, catching baby laughter on the air like delicate, iridescent bubbles. Thank you, Lord, for the gift of play returned to me in the hands of grandchildren. Keep me agile and ready to drop whatever task is tethering me to routine and follow where I am led, even across a goal line scuffed in the driveway dust.

Except ye be converted, and become as little children, ye shall not enter into the kingdom of heaven.

—Matthew 18:3

O Lord, what a blessing children are in this world. They bring such joy into our lives and are a precious composite of the best of our past and the hopes for the future. Thank you for your love for all children, Lord. Please guard them always.

Thou shalt rise up before the hoary head, and honour the face of the old man, and fear thy God: I am the Lord.

—Leviticus 19:32

Over the years, my siblings and I have sometimes drifted apart, not through animosity but because we've all been busy with our own immediate families. In dealing with our parents as they age and develop some health problems, we've moved back into a shared orbit. Thank you, God, for that newfound closeness as we navigate these sometimes daunting challenges together.

The Lord is the portion of mine inheritance and of my cup: thou maintainest my lot. The lines are fallen unto me in pleasant places; yea, I have a goodly heritage.

—Psalm 16:5–6

Today I thank you for my parents and grandparents, and all those people who taught me faith through their example. They modeled prayer and forgiveness and trust in you. I like to think I would have found my way to you, Lord, even without those gifts—or perhaps it's more that you would have found your way to me! But being brought up around faith-filled people made it easier when I had questions or problems or doubts. I want to pass on that faith to my children, and any friends or family members who look up to me.

December 10

> I would not have you to be ignorant, brethren, concerning them which are asleep, that ye sorrow not, even as others which have no hope. For if we believe that Jesus died and rose again, even so them also which sleep in Jesus will God bring with him.
>
> —1 Thessalonians 4:13-14

The year her husband died, Margaret almost didn't put the Christmas decorations out. Her grief was still fresh, and though she had muddled through Thanksgiving, she didn't know how she could get through the Christmas season. Right before Christmas, though, she found that the empty spaces bothered her more. She cried as she put the decorations out, remembering happier times when they had done so together, but she felt better for doing so. She found herself grateful—for the memories behind each ornament, for the friends who had made sure she was not alone during the season, and for God's presence during her time of grief.

Let us consider one another to provoke unto love and to good works: Not forsaking the assembling of ourselves together, as the manner of some is; but exhorting one another.

—Hebrews 10:24-25

Lord, I cannot thank you enough for my church community. When my husband was laid off unexpectedly last year, our stress levels were high and money was tight. Friends from church invited our kids along to some outings and quietly picked up the tab, helped my husband hone his resume, and rallied around in prayer. They were there for us during the hard times and they celebrated with us when he found a new job. Please bless them, God, for they demonstrated your love and support to us!

Watch ye, stand fast in the faith, quit you like men, be strong.

—1 Corinthians 16:13

Like a toddler who falls more than he stands, I'm pulling myself upright in the aftermath of death. I know you as a companion, God of mending hearts, and feel you steadying me. Thank you for the gift of resilience. Lead me to others who have hurt and gone on; I need to see how it's done.

Who his own self bare our sins in his own body on the tree, that we, being dead to sins, should live unto righteousness: by whose stripes ye were healed.

—1 Peter 2:24

Heavenly Spirit, I long to be healed from my affliction, but I trust your will, your timing, and your plan for my life. I know that you will never give me more than I can handle and that you will always be there to help me. For this I am eternally grateful. Amen.

With the ancient is wisdom; and in length of days understanding.

—Job 12:12

Where would we be without our elders? When I think about the people who came before me, I am filled with gratitude for their hard work and sacrifices. It is good to remember what they did and how they lived. Thank you, Lord, for giving us strong forebears who shaped the world and always looked toward creating a better future. Without them, my life would be very different. Help me appreciate and value the past.

For the wages of sin is death; but the gift of God is eternal life through Jesus Christ our Lord.

—Romans 6:23

Certain days, certain events come bounding into our way to remind us of how out of control life really is. It is then that we are most grateful for the angels that guard our way and guide our paths.

Jesus, thou joy of loving hearts!

Thou fount of life! Thou light of men!

From the best bliss that earth imparts,

We turn unfilled to thee again.

Thy truth unchanged hath ever stood;

Thou savest those that on thee call;

To them that seek thee, thou art good,

To them that find thee—All in All!

—12th-century prayer attributed to Bernard of Clairvaux

With all lowliness and meekness, with longsuffering, forbearing one another in love; Endeavouring to keep the unity of the Spirit in the bond of peace.

—Ephesians 4:2-3

Lord, how grateful I am to have found the love of my life. May I never take him for granted. May I focus on his strengths and be quick to forget any silly disagreement. Help me to be his encourager and his friend as well as his lover. Protect the bond between us, Lord. Keep it strong, healthy, and loving.

Provoke not your children to wrath: but bring them up in the nurture and admonition of the Lord.

—Ephesians 6:4

Thank you, God, that even when I fret, I know without a doubt that you are using my unique, special gifts and talents to nurture and teach my children. When I get down on myself and am unsure of my abilities, remind me that your commitment to me is lifelong.

When I was a child, I spake as a child, I understood as a child, I thought as a child: but when I became a man, I put away childish things.

—1 Corinthians 13:11

Thank you, Lord, for the gift of distance as children grow up and away. I'm ready to go on, too. My empty lap is eager for projects that will delight nest-flown children during brief stopovers, all of us too content going on to linger mournfully in our past.

Wherefore I also, after I heard of your faith in the Lord Jesus, and love unto all the saints, Cease not to give thanks for you, making mention of you in my prayers.

—Ephesians 1:15-16

When we give thanks and praise to someone, we honor the presence of God in that person. Our gratitude for the people we love is our acknowledgment of the Holy Spirit expressing through them. In all situations, let us express our gratitude to God.

A man that hath friends must shew himself friendly: and there is a friend that sticketh closer than a brother.

—Proverbs 18:24

Father, you help us to live gracefully by blessing us with wonderful friends. Thank you for making them as good as you are. Amen.

When thou makest a feast, call the poor, the maimed, the lame, the blind.

—Luke 14:13

You are a welcome guest at this table, God, as we pause in the midst of this bell-ringing, carol-making season of too much to do. Send us your gift of silent nights so that we can hear and know what you will be bringing us this year: yet another gift of hope. Bless our gathering around this table; we will set a place each day for you. Join us in our daily feast, for which we now give thanks. May it nourish our busy bodies as the anticipation of your presence among us does our weary spirits.

They gathered them together, and filled twelve baskets with the fragments of the five barley loaves, which remained over and above unto them that had eaten.

—John 6:13

God of providence, as I work to satisfy the hunger and thirst of my husband and children, I can feel your presence here in my kitchen, directing me and loving me. I remember with a thankful heart that you feed my family, too. I may appease their physical hunger, but you satisfy their hungry hearts with heavenly food—"the Bread of Life"—your son, Jesus Christ.

O Lord, who each day gives us our daily bread, bless my kitchen today as I use it to prepare nourishment for my family. My heart overflows as I joyfully cook and serve the meals in an act of love and worship.

Lord Jesus Christ, our Lord most dear,

as thou wast once an infant here,

so give this child of thine, we pray,

thy grace and blessing day by day.

O holy Jesus, Lord divine,

we pray thee guard this child of thine.

—Heinrich von Laufenberg, trans. Catherine Winkworth

The Christmas tree, O God, is groaning beneath gift-wrapped anticipation. The table spread before us is resplendent with shared foods prepared by loving hands, for which we give thanks. And now, as this waiting season ticks to a bell-ringing, midnight-marvelous close, we around this table are scooting over to make room for the anticipated Guest. Come, blessing us with the gift of your presence as we say, "Welcome."

Glory to God in the highest, and on earth peace, good will toward men.

—Luke 2:14

Merry Christmas! Thank you, Lord, for this special day. It is the birthday of your son, Jesus, and a bright and beautiful day for the world. Today I am grateful for rebirth, for celebrations, for sharing traditions with the people I love. Thank you for the gift of joy and new life.

Jesus saith unto him, I am the way, the truth, and the life: no man cometh unto the Father, but by me.

—John 14:6

Christ is born, go forth to meet Him,

Christ by all the heaven adored;

Singing songs of welcome, greet Him,

For the earth receives her Lord.

All ye nations, shout and sing;

For He comes, your glorious King.

—Traditional hymn

Thanks be to God, which giveth us the victory through our Lord Jesus Christ.

—1 Corinthians 15:57

Lord, how grateful we are that our spirits don't have to sag once the excitement of Christmas is over! We don't want to be like ungrateful children tearing through a pile of presents just to say, "Is that all?" For the gift you gave us at Christmas, your beloved son among us, is a gift that is ours all the days of our lives and throughout eternity! Thank you for the greatest gift of all, Lord.

Heaviness in the heart of man maketh it stoop: but a good word maketh it glad.

—Proverbs 12:25

The days after Christmas can sometimes be a bit of a letdown, but they can be peaceful, too. After all the preparation and rush, we have a little time to reflect and talk. Things that weren't "important" enough to get brought up at the big family meals make their way into conversation. Let me be grateful, Lord, for these gentle times of relaxation and renewal as we prepare for the end of the year.

But the mercy of the Lord is from everlasting to everlasting upon them that fear him, and his righteousness unto children's children; To such as keep his covenant, and to those that remember his commandments to do them.

—Psalm 103:17-18

Bless my family, O God, for it is unique... some say too much so. I am grateful you know we are joined by love—for each other and for and from you. We are grateful you use more than one pattern to create a good family. This pioneering family has you at its heart.

For the promise you unfold with the opening of each day, I thank you, Lord.

For blessings shared along the way, I thank you, Lord.

For the comfort of our home filled with love to keep us warm, I thank you, Lord.

For shelter from the winter storm, I thank you, Lord.

For the gifts of peace and grace you grant the family snug within, I thank you, Lord.

For shielding us from harm and sin, I thank you, Lord.

For the beauty of the snow sparkling in the winter sun, I thank you, Lord.

For the peace when the day is done, I thank you, Lord.

The sufferings of this present time are not worthy to be compared with the glory which shall be revealed in us.

—Romans 8:18

We're closing out the year tonight! Dear Lord, I ask for safety for my family and all friends and all those we love, both tonight as people attend celebrations and drive home, and in the year to come. I ask that I have a clear eye in the coming year to see all the ways in which you bless me abundantly. And I thank you for your love that surrounds me, enfolds me, and heals me. With you at my side, I am never alone.